Crescent Color Guide to
House Plants

Crescent Color Guide to

House Plants

Alan Titchmarsh

Crescent Books
New York

Copyright © The Hamlyn Publishing Group Limited MCMLXXXI

First English edition published by
The Hamlyn Publishing Group Limited
London · New York · Sydney · Toronto
Astronaut House, Feltham, Middlesex, England

Library of Congress Catalog Card Number:
ISBN 0-517-34186-7

This edition is published by Crescent Books,
a division of Crown Publishers, Inc.
a b c d e f g h

Printed in Italy

Photographic acknowledgments
Michael Plomer: pages 9 left, 13 right, 14, 15, 17–21, 22 left, 23–25, 26 left, 27, 29, 33, 36 left, 40, 41, 44, 45, 49, 54, 55, 62–67, 71–73, 78. Harry Smith: pages 7, 28, 30, 34, 35 right, 36 top, 38 top, 39, 42, 43, 52, 58, 70. Michael Warren: pages 37 bottom, 50, 51, 53, 77. Amateur Gardening: pages 74, 75, 79. The Hamlyn Group: pages 9 right, 10–12, 13 left, 16, 22 bottom, 26 left, 31, 32, 35 left, 38, 47, 48, 56, 57, 59, 61, 69.

Contents

Common Name Index

Latin names may seem a bore but they are standard and universal. For this reason all the plants have been listed under their latin names which are arranged alphabetically in each section. Beside each latin name is the plant's common name. Therefore, to find a plant you know by its common name, glance down this list to find its correct botanical name and then look it up in the appropriate section.

Key to plants: fo = popular foliage house plants; fl = popular flowering house plants; g = gift plants.

African violet, see *Saintpaulia* (fl)
Aluminium plant, see *Pilea* (fo)
Asparagus fern, see *Asparagus* (fo)
Azalea, see *Rhododendron* (g)
Balsam, see *Impatiens* (fl)
Bellflower, see *Campanula* (fl)
Bird's nest fern, see *Asplenium* (fo)
Bowstring hemp, see *Sansevieria* (fo)
Busy Lizzie, see *Impatiens* (fl)
Calamondin orange, see *Citrus* (fl)
Cape primrose, see *Streptocarpus* (fl)
Cast iron plant, see *Aspidistra* (fo)
Castor oil plant, False, see *Fatsia* (fo)
Christmas cactus, see *Schlumbergera* (fl)
Christmas pepper, see *Capsicum* (g)
Cigar plant, see *Cuphea* (fl)
Cineraria, see *Senecio* (g)
Clustered wax flower, see *Stephanotis* (fl)
Cordyline, see *Dracaena* (fo)
Creeping fig, see *Ficus* (fo)
Croton, see *Codiaeum* (fo)
Devil's ivy, see *Scindapsus* (fo)
Dragon tree, see *Dracaena* (fo)
Dumb cane, see *Dieffenbachia* (fo)
False aralia, see *Dizygotheca* (fo)
False castor oil plant, see *Fatsia* (fo)
Fat-headed Lizzie, see *Fatshedera* (fo)
Fern, see *Adiantum, Asplenium, Nephrolepis, Platycerium* (fo)
Fiddle-leaf fig, see *Ficus* (fo)
Fig-leaf palm, see *Fatsia* (fo)
Flame nettle, see *Coleus* (fo)
Flamingo flower, see *Anthurium* (fl)
Friendship plant, see *Pilea* (fo)
Geranium, see *Pelargonium* (fl)
Gloxinia, see *Sinningia* (g)
Grape ivy, see *Rhoicissus* (fo)
Herringbone plant, see *Maranta* (fo)
Honey plant, see *Hoya* (fl)
Inch plant, see *Tradescantia* and *Zebrina* (fo)
India rubber plant, see *Ficus* (fo)
Iron cross begonia, see *Begonia* (fo)
Ivy, see *Hedera* (fo)
Ivy tree, see *Fatshedera* (fo)
Japanese aralia, see *Fatsia* (fo)
Joseph's coat, see *Codiaeum* (fo)
Kangaroo vine, see *Cissus* (fo)
Kentia, see *Howea* (fo)

Ladder fern, see *Nephrolepis* (fo)
Leopard lily, see *Dieffenbachia* (fo)
Madagascar jasmine, see *Stephanotis* (fl)
Maidenhair fern, see *Adiantum* (fo)
Mexican breadfruit, see *Monstera* (fo)
Mother-in-law's tongue, see *Sansevieria* (fo)
Mother-of-thousands, see *Saxifraga* (fo)
Natal vine, see *Rhoicissus* (fo)
Neanthe, see *Chamaedorea* (fo)
Norfolk Island pine, see *Araucaria* (fo)
Orange tree, see *Citrus* (fl)
Palm, see *Chamaedorea* and *Howea* (fo)
Parasol plant, see *Heptapleurum* (fo)
Parlour palm, see *Aspidistra* (fo)
Patience plant, see *Impatiens* (fl)
Pepper, Ornamental, see *Capsicum* (g)
Poinsettia, see *Euphorbia* (g)
Prayer plant, see *Maranta* (fo)
Queen's tears, see *Billbergia* (fl)
Rubber plant, see *Ficus* (fo)
Saxifrage, see *Saxifraga* (fo)
Shingle plant, see *Monstera* (fo)
Shrimp plant, see *Beloperone* (fl)
Slipper flower, see *Calceolaria* (g)
Snakeskin plant, see *Fittonia* (fo)
Spanish bayonet, see *Yucca* (fo)
Spider plant, see *Chlorophytum* (fo)
Spiderwort, see *Tradescantia* (fo)
Stag's horn fern, see *Platycerium* (fo)
Star capsicum, see *Solanum* (g)
Star of Bethlehem, see *Campanula* (fl)
Strawberry geranium, see *Saxifraga* (fo)
Sweetheart plant, see *Philodendron* (fo)
Swiss cheese plant, see *Monstera* (fo)
Tail plant, see *Anthurium* (fl)
Ti tree, see *Yucca* (fo)
Umbrella plant, see *Cyperus* (fo)
Umbrella tree, see *Heptapleurum* (fo)
Urn plant, see *Aechmea* (fo)
Vase plant, see *Aechmea* (fo)
Wandering jew, see *Tradescantia* and *Zebrina* (fo)
Wandering sailor, see *Tradescantia* and *Zebrina* (fo)
Wax flower, see *Hoya* (fl)
Weeping fig, see *Ficus* (fo)
Winter cherry, see *Solanum* (g)
Zebra plant, see *Aphelandra* (fl)
Zygocactus, see *Schlumbergera* (fl)

Choosing the Right Plant

There are so many house plants available for sale nowadays that buying one is as complicated as buying a car. Which model will serve you best? Which will be the right size? Which will you be able to afford?

First ask yourself whether you want a plant that will be a permanent resident in your home or a short-term guest. Most foliage plants fall into the first category, and most flowering plants, because of their shorter life span, fall into the second. If you are cunning you can search out plants which flower but which also carry reasonably pleasant foliage all the year round.

It is not only the size of a plant which determines its cost, often its rate of growth has a direct bearing on the matter. Some large and slow-growing palms can cost £50 or more while a simple spider plant would be about 50p. Whatever its cost it is always best to choose a plant that is well suited to the environment you have to offer and to the space available. Will a tall plant look best, or should it be bushy? Trailers will look good if they are given room to trail, climbers will need some kind of vertical support system. Small rosette-forming plants will fit anywhere provided that prevailing conditions suit them.

Most house plants sold in the United Kingdom are natives of warmer countries. Some even come from the tropics, so it is important to provide them with suitable temperatures and the correct light intensity as well as reasonable humidity and air circulation. If all this sounds rather technical the following lists should help to make the choice of plant easier. Whatever the prevailing conditions in your rooms, there is a house plant that will grow well in almost any situation. All you have to do is find it!

FOR SHADY CORNERS
Asparagus, aspidistra, asplenium, fatshedera, fatsia, fittonia, maranta, nephrolepis, philodendron, rhoicissus and *sansevieria* are the plants to choose. However, even plants which tolerate shade will enjoy a little indirect light if this can be provided.

FOR GOOD BUT INDIRECT LIGHT
Adiantum, aechmea, araucaria, asparagus, begonia, beloperone, chamaedorea, chlorophytum, cissus, codiaeum, coleus, cyperus, dieffenbachia, dizygotheca, dracaena, ficus, hedera, heptapleurum, howea, monstera, peperomia, pilea, platycerium, tradescantia, yucca, zebrina and most flowering pot plants. Remember that the majority of house plants thrive in this situation.

The Asparagus fern, *Asparagus plumosus*, will grow well in good light or shade.

FOR SUNNY SPOTS
Beloperone, billbergia, citrus, coleus, pelargonium, sansevieria, tradescantia and *zebrina* all do well in the sun but even these plants will be scorched by really bright sun if it shines on them for most of the day.

FOR WARM BATHROOMS
Adiantum, aechmea, anthurium, aphelandra, billbergia, codiaeum, cyperus, dieffenbachia, dracaena, nephrolepis, platycerium, saintpaulia and *scindapsus.* All these plants like humidity so if you grow them elsewhere provide atmospheric moisture by spraying with water or standing the plant pots on moist gravel.

FOR UNHEATED ROOMS
Araucaria, aspidistra, beloperone, billbergia, calceolaria, campanula, chlorophytum, chrysanthemum, citrus, cyclamen, fatshedera, fatsia, hedera, hydrangea, pelargonium, rhoicissus, rhododendron, saxifraga and *senecio.* Most of these plants actually enjoy being cool so keep them away from heaters.

FOR CENTRALLY HEATED ROOMS
Aechmea, aspidistra, begonia, chlorophytum, cissus, dieffenbachia, dracaena, ficus, hedera, heptapleurum, hoya, howea, maranta, monstera, peperomia, philodendron, rhoicissus, saintpaulia, sansevieria and *tradescantia.* Never stand plants directly over or against radiators or heaters – they will be scorched and the leaves will drop.

Having decided on the plant you need, the next step is to find it. Without doubt, the best place to buy a plant is in the nursery where it was grown, for you can transport it direct to your home with as little disturbance as possible. Garden centres are the next best, for the plants should at least be warm and cosy inside a greenhouse, even if it is not the one they were originally raised in. Buy from multiple stores only when the plants are known to be fresh and when they look in the peak of condition. The worst place to buy is from greengrocers who let the plants stand outside on a draughty pavement. They are bound to have suffered a check to their growth and may shed leaves or wilt as a result. It is better to pay a little more for a plant that you know is going to survive than to save money on a poor, doomed specimen.

Buy for preference in spring and summer when weather conditions are at their most favourable for plant growth. However, many winter-flowering plants are only offered for sale in the darker months of the year and will have to be bought at that time.

When choosing a plant from any sales outlet make sure of the following points:

1 The plant should be of a good shape with no wilting leaves. Avoid tall and spindly specimens.

2 There should be no evidence of pests and diseases and the leaves should be healthy and unmarked (unless the markings are part of their attraction).

3 The compost in the pot should be moist and there should be no gap between the compost and the side of the pot.

4 Flowering plants should be chosen with some blooms open, yet some still in bud. If in full flower they will go over quickly and if the buds are too tightly closed they may never open in their new environment.

Wherever you buy the plant, insist that it is properly wrapped up in paper for the journey home. This will prevent damage to the leaves and stems by bruising, and will also keep the plant warmer in winter. If the plant is taken home by car do not leave it unsupported in the boot. Neither leave it for hours in a parked car in sunny weather.

Careful selection and transport will help to ensure survival, but for the first few days keep any foliage plant in a reasonably warm (but not hot) room and in good but indirect light. The plant needs just a little time to settle down so do not be alarmed if it loses a few leaves in the first week or two.

Popular Foliage House Plants

Adiantum (Maidenhair fern)

A supremely graceful plant with wafer-thin foliage that looks like finely cut fresh-green tissue paper. The wiry black stems arch gently and the fronds flutter in the slightest movement of air. The brown spots on the underside of each frond are spore cases so do not be alarmed by their presence. *Adiantum capillus-veneris* is the easiest species to cultivate.

In the right situation the Maidenhair fern will grow to a height of 18 in (45 cm) and as much across. It abhors dry air and bright sunshine, preferring a more humid and indirectly lit situation. It also likes a peaty compost that is kept moist at all times. Feed once a month from May to September and repot in spring when the plant has outgrown its container. Dead fronds can be cut out as they fade and if you are feeling brave, large plants can be divided to make several smaller specimens in the spring.

A temperature of around 50–60°F (10–16°C) suits it, and it will enjoy being stood on a tray of moist gravel. Never spray it with insecticide which will cause the fronds to turn brown.

A humid atmosphere is what the Maidenhair fern needs if its fronds are to stay fresh and green.

Aechmea (Urn plant; Vase plant)

The Urn plant gets its name from the vase-like arrangement of its leaves which are spiny-edged and speckled with white meal. Out of the centre of the rosette will emerge a large, spiky flowerhead with pink bracts and blue flowers. This inflorescence will last for months, but when it does fade, so too will the large rosette, eventually to be replaced by a number of smaller ones.

Water the plant actually into the rosette – keeping the vase partially full at all times. Temperatures between 50–80°F (10–27°C) are tolerated, but the higher temperature is better if you are trying to induce flowering. The plant grows to a height of about 1 ft (30 cm) and enjoys a position in light shade or good but indirect light. From May to September spray the leaves daily with water and add some diluted foliar feed to the water once a month to give the plant a boost.

Keep the centre of the Urn plant full of water and the flower spike will last for many weeks.

Avoid growing any bromeliads (plants of the pineapple family) in overlarge pots; they have small root systems and resent too much compost. Repot only when the plant is obviously starved or when the pot is too small to hold it upright. When the central rosette fades the young ones that replace it should be separated and potted up individually in small containers of a peat-based potting compost.

Araucaria (Norfolk Island pine)

A smaller relation of the Monkey puzzle tree, *Araucaria excelsa* has all of its relation's symmetrical grace. The spiky bright green branches emerge at regular intervals up the stem, making the plant a valuable focal point in any room.

This plant enjoys light shade or indirect light such as that received through a north-facing window. It prefers cool rooms with temperatures of between 50–60°F (10–16°C) and likes to stand on a tray of moist gravel or be given a daily spray of tepid water. It will eventually reach a height of around 5 ft (1.5 m) and should be repotted in John Innes No. 3 potting compost or another loam-based compost every two or three years. Soak the compost whenever it shows signs of becoming dry for the plant will shed its needles if left bone dry for any length of time. Feed every two weeks from May to September. The compost can be allowed to remain a little drier in winter when growth slows down. Propagation is by means of seeds (which can be bought rather than produced by potted plants) and by taking a cutting of the growing point, though only aged and unsightly plants should be butchered in this way.

Asparagus (Asparagus fern)

There are two distinct kinds of Asparagus fern. *Asparagus plumosus* is the wispy type that is used as a backing for carnations in wedding buttonholes. It has wiry, upright stems about 18 in (45 cm) tall on which the flat fronds are carried almost at right angles. *Asparagus sprengeri* has a fuzzy appearance and more of an arching, pendant habit than *plumosus*. In spite of their appearance, neither of the plants is a true fern and they are consequently rather easier to grow than those humidity-loving plants.

Both enjoy light shade or diffused light. Bright sunlight leads to scorching and subsequent shedding of 'needles'. A temperature of between 50–70°F (10–21°C) keeps them happy. The compost can be allowed to dry out between waterings, but take care not to leave it bone dry for too long or the fronds will turn yellow, once again dropping their needles. Feed once every two weeks from May to September and repot each spring into a peat-based compost. Both plants can be divided up at potting time when they are overcrowded and more plants are wanted, and both grow easily from seeds.

Known to the Victorians as the Cast iron plant, the aspidistra will survive in any home provided it is not overwatered.

Aspidistra (Cast iron plant; Parlour palm)
This plant's common name ought to inspire the laziest gardeners. It thrives on neglect and whenever problems are encountered they are usually attributable to over-generosity. The glossy pointed leaves arch elegantly from the soil and are a deep shade of green. There is also a cream-striped variety 'Variegata' but this is harder to find than the plain type and also harder to grow. In time the aspidistra will make a massive clump (the individual leaves last for years) and may stand as much as 2 ft (60 cm) high. Temperatures between 50–70°F (10–21°C) suit both types.

An assortment of ferns looks very much at home in the shady arbour provided by an unused fireplace.

This superb Bird's nest fern needs a daily spray of tepid water to keep it in peak condition.

Although it will tolerate reasonable, though not bright, sunlight, the main value of the plant lies in its ability to tolerate heavy shade and it can be relied upon to thrive in dark corners. The most important part of its cultivation is watering. It will withstand being dry at the roots for several weeks, but it will *not* put up with soggy compost that never dries out. For this reason, always use John Innes potting compost or another loam-based compost which can be allowed to dry out without shrinking from the sides of the pot. Repotting is another thing the aspidistra dislikes. Repot only when the plant is really overcrowded and has no more room to send up leaves. Feed every two weeks through the summer and divide the plant in spring to propagate stock for your friends . . . or for other dark corners.

Asplenium (Bird's nest fern)

The bright green shuttlecock of shiny leaves, each one centred with a brown rib, makes *Asplenium nidus* almost totally irresistible when it is seen in peak condition. The fleshy fronds will reach a height of around 2 ft (60 cm) in well-grown mature specimens, and the secret of keeping a smart plant without brown edges is to provide a humid environment.

Either stand the plant pot on a tray of gravel which is kept constantly moist, or give it a daily (or twice-daily) spray with tepid rainwater. Most ferns enjoy reasonable but indirect light (not heavy shade) and like the peaty compost in the pot to be kept moist at all times. This plant is no exception to the rule, but avoid keeping the compost soggy – it wants to be moist, not wet. Room temperatures of between 50–70°F (10–21°C) are put up with quite happily. Any necessary repotting can be carried out in spring using a peat-based compost or John Innes with a little peat added.

Scale insects can be a problem. They fasten themselves to the undersides of the fronds and look like little legless tortoises. Avoid using chemical sprays which may burn the fronds. Instead, sponge the pests off with a wad of moist cotton wool.

Because the plant forms a symmetrical rosette, vegetative propagation is inadvisable. Spores can be sown when they are produced, but this, too, is a chancy business. The best course of action is to buy a young plant and grow it on.

Begonia

Indoor gardeners who are tired of green leaves can have a field day with the various varieties of *Begonia rex*. Here the large, pointed leaves are coloured silver, maroon, pale green and crimson in an assortment of patterns. *Begonia masoniana* (the iron cross begonia) has rough-textured green leaves on which appears a dark brown replica of the German war decoration. The plants grow 9 in (23 cm) or so high.

Both these begonias, and also the tall pink-flowered types with silver-spotted foliage, enjoy good but indirect light and temperatures between 60–70°F (16–21°C). Water the compost when it feels dry, and feed the plants every two weeks from May to September. Overwatering will cause the stems to rot. Stand the pots on moist gravel to prevent leaf scorch.

Repot each spring in John Innes potting compost or another loam-based compost, but do not be surprised if the rex begonias pass away after a couple of years – they are sometimes shortlived in the home. Propagate by leaf cuttings to keep them going.

Begonia rex is available in a wide variety of foliage variegations that include shades of red, maroon, green and silver.

Chamaedorea (Palm)

This miniature palm is ideal where space is in short supply, for it has all the grace of a full-sized palm tree but only grows to a height of 3 ft (1 m) and that extremely slowly. It is sold under the name of *Chamaedorea elegans* or *Neanthe bella* and makes a good room or bottle garden plant.

Light or heavy shade is tolerated, but bright sunshine tends to burn the leaf tips. Temperatures between 50–65°F (10–18°C) are most suitable. Water this little palm with care – allowing the compost to dry out between waterings, though not to the extent of being dust dry. Feed every two weeks in summer. An occasional spray with tepid water will be enjoyed, and the leaves can be wiped clean when they are dusty. Repot only when the roots have outgrown the available space and then use John Innes potting compost or another loam-based compost. Propagation is by seed which will have to be bought. Young plants are a cheap and more reliable means of increase if only one or two are required.

Chlorophytum (Spider plant)

Ease of cultivation and a handsome habit of growth make the spider plant a popular choice. The leaves are attractively striped cream and green and both white flowers and young plantlets are carried at the ends of long, arching, cream-coloured stems.

Give the plant good light but keep it out of direct sunshine which may scorch the leaves. Water it as soon as the compost is dry in spring and summer and keep it just a little drier at the roots in winter. Feed every two weeks from April to September. Feeding is very important, for starved plants develop brown leaf tips. Repot every spring into John Innes or a peat-based potting compost so that the plant is well supplied with nutrients. It tolerates a wide range of temperatures; from 45–70°F (7–21°C). The stems with plantlets are produced by mature plants, so be patient. The offspring can be cut off and potted up individually in 3-in (8-cm) pots of compost.

Give Joseph's coat good light, warmth and humidity to make sure that it keeps all its leaves.

Cissus (Kangaroo vine)

Though the foliage of *Cissus antarctica* is just plain green, the scalloped edges, the glossy surface to each leaf and the clambering habit make it a pleasing plant, especially useful for dimly lit corners. It puts up quite happily with shade, though indirect light is likely to produce a better-shaped plant, and it enjoys temperatures as low as 45°F (7°C). Give it a tripod of canes or some other framework over which to scramble and it can reach a height of several feet. Water when dry and feed every two weeks through the summer. Repot each spring and propagate by stem cuttings at the same time.

Codiaeum (Joseph's coat)

Often referred to as 'crotons', this group of plants possesses a wide range of spectacular foliage variegations in shades of red, orange, yellow and green. Unfortunately, they are not the easiest of plants to grow, but with a little effort they can be encouraged to thrive.

Position the plant in good light – not in shade or scorching sun. Keep temperatures between 60–75°F (16–24°C). Spray the plant daily with tepid rainwater or stand it on a bed of moist gravel. Keep the compost gently moist through spring and summer (a little drier in winter) and feed every two weeks from spring to autumn. These simple rules are the secrets of success. If you keep the plant in conditions which are too cool or let it go short of food and water, the lower leaves are likely to fall.

If you want to make a bushy specimen, pinch out the growing point. Repot in spring when necessary, and propagate by stem cuttings kept in a temperature of around 70°F (21°C).

15

Coleus (Flame nettle)

The vividly-coloured strains of coleus with their red, orange, yellow, green and plum-purple leaf markings are probably best regarded as annuals which can be replaced each spring. They are easy to grow during summer when light and heat are freely available, but can be difficult to grow well through the winter.

Coleus need ample supplies of water – the leaves will quickly wilt when the compost is dry – and should be fed every two weeks from April to September. They insist on good light and will tolerate full sun for all or part of the day. Pinch out the shoot tips to encourage bushiness, and remove any developing flowers which will slow down growth. The plant will grow to between 1–2 ft (30–60 cm) tall depending on the size of pot in which it is grown. If started in a 3-in or 4-in (8-cm or 10-cm) pot in spring it should be moved on to a 5-in (12-cm) pot in summer.

Through the winter make sure that the plant has as light a place as possible and a minimum temperature of 50°F (10°C). Cut it back in spring and take stem cuttings to make replacement plants.

Cyperus (Umbrella plant)

There are two species of umbrella plant, *Cyperus diffusus* and *Cyperus alternifolius*. Both are handsome plants with rosettes of leaves carried like umbrella spokes at the top of stiff stems, but *C. diffusus* grows to around 1 ft (30 cm) or so, while *C. alternifolius* may be anything from 3–6 ft (1–2 m). Both can carry brown grassy flowers among their spokes in summer.

Both types enjoy good indirect light or gentle shade and will tolerate temperatures as low as 50°F (10°C). They grow in very moist soil in their natural environment so the compost in the pot should never be allowed to dry out. Stand the pot in a shallow bowl and keep this constantly full of water. Spray the leaves occasionally with tepid water. Remove stems completely as they fade, and repot the plant each spring into John Innes or a soilless mixture. Propagation is by division at repotting time.

Dieffenbachia (Dumb cane)

Exotic-looking plants with large oval leaves spotted with silver, cream or white. The common name is derived from the unpleasant effect the sap has on the tongue, though its alternative common name of Leopard lily is perhaps more pleasantly informative.

Below: Dizygotheca, the False aralia, is unsurpassed when it comes to delicacy of foliage.

Right: Just one of the many foliage variations in the colourful coleus.

16

The cream-splashed leaves of the Dumb cane make a pleasant change from other green-leaved house plants.

The plant will reach a height of 2 ft (60 cm) or more and likes to be kept moist (not wet) at the roots at all times. It enjoys gentle shade or indirect light. Let the compost dry out a little between watering in winter. Keep the plant warm and maintain a winter minimum temperature of 55–60°F (13–16°C). Spray the foliage daily with tepid water, and feed the plant every two weeks from May to September. Repot in spring when necessary, using a peat-based potting compost. Old plants can be cut hard back at the same time and stem cuttings rooted in a warm, humid environment.

Dizygotheca (False aralia)

This is a very pretty plant with starry, jagged-edged leaves of dark brown. It will eventually grow to a height of around 6 ft (2 m) in the home and 20 ft (6 m) or more in a greenhouse. It is exceptionally handsome.

Having said that, it is not too easy to grow! Give it a spot in good, indirect light, and water it well as soon as the compost feels dry to the touch. If it is kept too wet or too dry, the plant will shed its leaves. Feed every two weeks in summer. A warm room is appreciated with a minimum temperature of 60°F (16°C), and daily misting with a hand sprayer will keep the air nice and moist.

Right: Perhaps the most graceful of the figs, the Weeping fig is a beautiful plant for a spot in good but indirect light.

Below: With a name like the Dragon tree you would expect leaves that are brightly coloured. Some varieties have green and yellow stripes.

Above: Reputedly a cross between fatsia and ivy, fatshedera looks like an exact combination of its two parents.

Tall specimens can be cut back to leave a 6-in (15-cm) stump in spring, but propagation is rather difficult; settle for buying a small plant and growing it on. Repot in John Innes compost or a commercial potting mix every couple of years during summer.

Dracaena (Dragon tree; Cordyline)
These come in all sorts of foliage variegations (red, maroon, cream, yellow and green) but all possess a stately fountain of leaves on top of a stiff stem. They will reach a height of between 2–4 ft (60–125 cm) in the home.

Keep the plants warm (with a minimum temperature of 55°F (13°C), and in light shade. Allow the compost to dry out slightly between waterings, and then give a good soak. Feed every two weeks in summer. Repot in spring into John Innes or a peat-based potting compost. A daily misting with tepid water will keep the plants happy and prevent tip-burn on the leaves.

Propagation is by air layering or the removal of thick and fleshy roots known as 'toes'. These are potted up individually and grown on in a warm, light place.

Fatshedera (Fat-headed Lizzie; Ivy tree)
A cross between Ivy (*Hedera*) and the Fig-leaf palm (*Fatsia*), this plant has the climbing tendencies of one parent and the leaf shape of the other.

It is a fine subject for a cool room in good light or light shade, and can either be trained up canes to a height of several feet, or else allowed to trail. Alternatively, pinch out the shoot tips at around 1 ft (30 cm) to keep the plant bushy. Keep the compost gently moist at all times and feed every two weeks in summer. Repot in spring when necessary. There is a variegated variety which is not too easy to find and a little more difficult to grow. Propagation is by stem cuttings which can be easily rooted in summer.

Fatsia (Fig-leaf palm; Japanese aralia)
A superb plant for beginners and idle gardeners, the Fig-leaf palm has large, glossy, hand-shaped leaves and makes a rounded or upright bush. It tolerates good light or shade equally well and thrives in unheated rooms. It is often grown in gardens and so can stand a fair degree of frost.

Water the compost well as soon as it starts to dry out, and feed every two weeks in summer. Repot in spring when necessary. Pinching out of the shoot tips will keep the plant within bounds, but it can always be planted out in the garden when it becomes too large for your rooms.

Propagation is by seeds or by stem cuttings – both methods are best carried out in spring or summer.

Ficus (Fig; Rubber plant)

The true, edible fig is seldom grown as a house plant, but many of its relatives are. The most common is the Rubber plant with its tall, sentry-stiff stem and oval, pointed leaves of shining dark green. Much more interesting are its variegated varieties *Ficus elastica* 'Tricolor' and *F.e.* 'Variegata'. Possessing grace lacked by the Rubber plant, and gaining in popularity, is the weeping fig, *Ficus benjamina*; a superbly elegant plant with gently-weeping grey-barked branches and oval mid-green leaves. Creeping figs such as *Ficus pumila* have still smaller leaves and are rather more difficult to grow than their taller relations – they require warm rooms, shade and a moist atmosphere if they are not to shrivel and turn brown.

The False castor oil, or fatsia, makes a bold show and can be planted in the garden when it grows too large for the house.

The big brothers enjoy good but indirect light, and a good soaking every time the compost dries out. Over-watering is a common cause of failure, for the leaves turn yellow and fall if the roots are too wet. Temperatures as low as 45°F (7°C) are tolerated (though not particularly enjoyed). The two larger species mentioned can reach 8 ft (2.5 m) in good conditions, as can the leathery-leaved Fiddle-leaf fig, *Ficus lyrata*.

Feed all the figs every two weeks in summer, and repot in John Innes potting compost No. 2 or 3 or another loam-based compost every other spring (soilless compost is not heavy enough to hold them upright). A daily misting is greatly to the liking of the weeping fig, and do not be alarmed if this species sheds a few leaves shortly after being introduced to your room. This is quite usual and does not last for long.

Propagation is by leaf cuttings or air layering for the Rubber plant, air layering for the Fiddle-leaf fig, and by stem cuttings for the other types. The Rubber plant can be cut back in spring if it grows too large – the stump that is left will soon produce a bushy head of branches.

Fittonia (Snakeskin plant)

The fittonias are a lovely group of low-growing plants with delicately marked leaves, the veins being either pink or cream, but they have a reputation for being difficult to grow indoors. The larger-leaved varieties need warmth (a minimum temperature of 60°F (16°C) is essential), some shade from bright sun, and constant humidity. Bed the pot into a shallow dish of moist gravel or peat for best results, and mist the leaves occasionally with water. Pinch out the tips of any straggly shoots.

Much easier to grow, but no less decorative, is a smaller-leaved variety called *Fittonia argyroneura* 'Nana'. It will tolerate a dry atmosphere more readily and should survive in most rooms. Give all types a good watering when they are dry, keeping them gently moist through the summer but drier in winter. Feed monthly in summer; repot in spring if necessary in a peat-based compost, and propagate by division at the same time.

Hedera (Ivy)

As trailers or climbers these perform well indoors. They are available in seemingly limitless variegations and leaf shapes to bring brightness and interest to corners where other, more demanding, plants may be difficult to grow. *Hedera helix* is the most common species and the one with relatively small leaves. Among its best varieties for indoor growing are 'Glacier', edged with white; 'Little Diamond', diamond-shaped leaves edged with white, and 'Parsley Crested' with green, crinkly-edged leaves. Larger and more spectacularly variegated foliage is to be found on *Hedera canariensis* 'Gloire de Marengo', the leaves being splashed with creamy yellow.

Provide the plants with a tripod of canes or some other support, or allow the varieties of *Hedera helix* to trail. They all prefer cool rooms and may be unhappy with overpowering central heating. Position them in good, but indirect light or gentle shade, and soak the compost as soon as the surface feels dry to the touch. A daily misting will keep the foliage fresh and discourage red spider mite which is often a problem on ivies in a dry atmosphere. Feed every two weeks in summer and repot in spring if necessary. Propagate by stem cuttings in summer. Plant the small-leaved varieties in the garden when they outgrow your rooms.

Heptapleurum (Umbrella tree; Parasol plant)

On good specimens, the plant's firm, unbranched stem is clothed from top to bottom with many-fingered green leaves and may reach a height of 6 ft (2 m) or more. If the top is pinched out, the plant can be encouraged to become bushy.

Give it a spot in good but indirect light in a warm room with a minimum temperature of 55°F (13°C). It likes a good soaking once the surface of the compost feels dry to the touch, but can be kept a little drier in winter than in summer. Occasional misting is beneficial and repotting should be carried out in spring every year or so. Feed every two weeks from May to September. Propagation is by means of stem cuttings or seeds.

Howea (Palm; Kentia)

The two *Howea* species, *H. belmoreana* and *H. forsteriana* are spectacular palms which are not too difficult to grow in most homes. Their arching stems and leaves bring a real 'palm court' flavour to any room, and they may reach a height of 6 ft (2 m) and more.

Fittonia argyroneura nana is by far the easiest of the Snakeskin plants to care for.

The red-veined fittonia in this bowl arrangement (front) will enjoy the company of its humidity-loving neighbours – a dracaena, a weeping fig and some ivy – but such plantings must be regarded as temporary.

Below: The elegant Umbrella tree.

Left: The howea palm tree is supremely stately but also rather expensive due to its slow rate of growth.

Their slow rate of growth makes them expensive to buy, so make sure you provide the right conditions to ensure their survival. They like moderate warmth (minimum 50°F) (10°C) and indirect light or gentle shade. They do not enjoy bright sunlight which may scorch the tips of the leaves. Soak the compost thoroughly only when it is dry – palms do not like to be too wet at the roots. Mist the leaves occasionally and wipe them clean of any dust from time to time. Repot in John Innes potting compost No. 2 or 3 or another loam-based compost only when the plant has become really root-bound, and then ensure that drainage is excellent and that the compost is well firmed. Feed monthly in summer and propagate by shop-bought seed to raise your own plants. High temperatures need to be maintained in the early stages of growth.

Maranta (Prayer plant; Herringbone plant)

The marantas are a beautifully marked race of plants, their green leaves being blotched or striped with brown, red or white, but they are a little tricky to cultivate. All are low-growing or slightly bushy.

To keep them happy they must be kept warm at all times – especially in winter – and protected from the rays of the sun. A spot in light shade suits them best and they can be bedded in a tray of moist peat or gravel so that the atmosphere around their leaves is constantly humid. Water with care and soak the compost when it shows signs of drying out. Do not keep the plants too wet or they may rot off. Feed once a month in summer. Repot in spring when the plant has filled its container, and propagate by division at the same time.

Monstera (Swiss cheese plant)

Deservedly a popular house plant, the Swiss cheese plant, also known as the Shingle plant or Mexican breadfruit, is a stately specimen for larger rooms where it can be allowed to spread itself. The thick, questing stems support massive heart-shaped leaves that are slashed and holed on mature plants, and it dangles long aerial roots towards the soil. The plant will reach 8 ft (2.5 m) and more when it is happy.

Give your plant a good-sized pot so that it is not short of nutrients, and position it in good indirect light. Lack of either requirement is likely to result in plants with unperforated leaves. Support the stem on a stout stake or cane and lead the aerial roots to the compost – do not cut them off. Maintain a minimum temperature of around 50°F (10°C) and mist the leaves occasionally. The compost should be allowed to dry out slightly between waterings and liquid feed can be given every week from May to September. Repot each spring into John Innes potting compost with extra peat added or another loam-based compost. If the plant outgrows its space it can be cut back to a healthy leaf and encouraged to bush out. Propagation is by air layering or by rooting shoot tips that are removed to encourage bushiness. Carry out both operations in spring.

Nephrolepis (Ladder fern)

This bright green fern with its fountain of fronds is so tempting when seen in nurseries and multiple stores at the peak of perfection that it is snapped up by plant lovers, but, so often when it is brought home, the fronds turn brown and drop off. The secret of success is really quite simple. Keep the plant moderately warm – between 50–70°F (10–21°C) is a suitable range –

Below: Ladder ferns need plenty of humidity, and a good spray over with tepid water every day will help to keep them fresh.

Right: The Prayer plant is so named because of its habit of folding its leaves together at night.

Far right: Although small at the outset, the Swiss cheese plant will grow as high as your rooms if conditions are right for it.

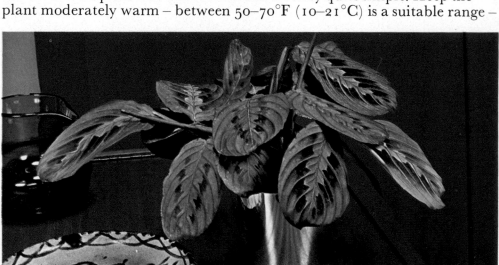

and in good, but indirect light – not heavy shade. The peaty compost should never be allowed to dry out but on the other hand, it should not be kept saturated. As soon as it shows the slightest suspicion of being dry give it a good soak. Spray the plant daily with tepid water. Repot every spring into a peat-based compost and, if you want to increase your stock, divide the plant at the same time. Atmospheric dryness is the main enemy of the plant, so it is important to keep it out of draughts and away from radiators and other heat sources. Cut off any fronds that are yellow or faded and feed occasionally in summer.

Peperomia

An attractive bunch of plants growing to little more than 6 in (15 cm) high and possessing finely marked leaves and sometimes little poker-shaped flower spikes. *Peperomia magnoliifolia* has glossy cream and green oval leaves; those of *P. caperata* are dark green and heavily corrugated, and *P. argyreia* has green leaves striped with silver-grey.

All enjoy a warm room with the lowest temperature being 55°F (13°C) and a position in good, indirect light or gentle shade. Allow the compost to dry out between waterings – a common cause of failure is over-watering which causes stem rot. Feed every two weeks through the summer and repot in spring only if the plant has outgrown its container. Propagation is by stem cuttings or, for the stemless varieties, by leaf cuttings – both can be taken in spring and summer.

Philodendron (Sweetheart plant)

There are many plants in this family with an assortment of leaf shapes. Most of them climb eagerly up a cane or moss-covered stick. The most popular is undoubtedly the Sweetheart plant *Philodendron scandens* on which the glossy green leaves are shaped like hearts. This species can be allowed to trail where there is no room for it to climb, but larger-leaved varieties like *P. hastatum* must be given some support.

Both plants enjoy a spot in a warm room where temperatures are unlikely to fall below 55°F (13°C), and both grow well in good, indirect light or gentle shade; *P. scandens* will also thrive in very dark corners if its other requirements can be met. These are given a good soaking when the compost feels dry to the touch, and a feed every two weeks in summer. Mist the foliage daily and repot every couple of years in a peat-based compost. Cuttings are easy to root in summer.

Pilea (Aluminium plant; Friendship plant)

The aluminium plant, *Pilea cadierei* 'Nana', is a low-growing subject well suited to being used in plant arrangements and bottle gardens. Its oval leaves are green and blotched with silver grey. The friendship plant is *P. involucrata* which has dark brown leaves, again silver blotched. *P.* 'Moon Valley' has rough-textured green leaves tinged with plum-purple.

Peperomia argyreia – a colourful potful for a confined space.

Right: The Sweet-heart plant (seen here with a Christmas cactus) makes a handsome column of glossy foliage in reasonable light or shade.

Below: *Philodendron hastatum* grown in a hydroculture unit.

Below: Not very common, but remarkably attractive, is *Pilea* 'Moon Valley'.

Right: One of the easiest of all house plants is the Grape ivy – it grows in good light or heavy shade.

Above: The Stag's horn fern looks best when mounted on a branch or a piece of cork bark.

All three are valuable and easy-to-grow plants where space is limited. They require a reasonably warm room of at least 50°F (10°C) and good indirect light or gentle shade. Water thoroughly when dry, but then allow to dry out once more. Feed every two weeks in summer. Occasional misting is beneficial and annual repotting can be carried out in spring. Propagate by stem cuttings in spring and summer; the removal of these shoot tips will help to keep the plants bushy.

Platycerium (Stag's horn fern)

This weird-looking plant makes a good talking point, for a well-grown specimen is a handsome sight which closely resembles the hunting trophy from which it takes its common name.

Cultivation is as for *Nephrolepis* which has been previously described but this fern can be mounted on a piece of cork bark, its roots surrounded by sphagnum moss and its brown pad, which should never be tampered with, held against the bark with wire. Cork bark is obtainable from your nurseryman or garden centre. Twice weekly dunkings in a bucket of water will keep the fern moist at the roots, and it can be hung in a spot that receives reasonable light.

Rhoicissus (Grape ivy; Natal vine)

This must be the top plant as far as ease of cultivation goes. The Grape ivy produces many climbing or scrambling stems clad in glossy green leaves with scalloped edges and will reach a height of 6 ft (2 m) and more if trained up a tripod of canes or some other support. It is also available in a variety which is commercially referred to as 'Ellen Danica'. Here the leaves are slitted and take on a more finely cut appearance.

26

Water the plant thoroughly when the compost feels dry, and feed every two weeks in summer. Keep it in good indirect light or a shady corner. In both situations it will tolerate a wide range of temperatures, provided a minimum of 45°F (7°C) can be assured. It can be drastically thinned and cut back in spring when it is overgrown, and the material removed can be turned into cuttings. Repot each spring for best results.

Sansevieria (Mother-in-law's tongue; Bowstring hemp)

Another fail-safe pot plant, *Sansevieria trifasciata* 'Laurentii' is the 3-ft (1-m) tall, spiky-leaved Mother-in-law's tongue. It has green and grey marbled leaves which are edged with butter yellow.

Maintain a minimum temperature of 50°F (10°C) and keep the plant in good light – bright sun if you like. Allow the compost in the pot to become bone dry between waterings and do not repot the plant until it cracks its existing pot. It will perform best when rootbound and likes John Innes or another loam-based compost rather than soilless mixes. A soilless mix may also prove too light to hold the plant upright. Propagation is by removal and individual potting of the rooted leaves or 'offsets'.

In spite of its common name, the Mother-in-law's tongue is a pleasant plant. It enjoys a hot and sunny spot.

Saxifraga (Mother-of-thousands; Strawberry geranium)

Saxifraga stolonifera is a modest little pot plant with miniature offspring at the ends of fine, trailing runners. The leaves may be green, veined with grey, and spotted pink on the underside, and in the variety 'Tricolor' they are variegated green, white and rosy pink.

This plant needs a shelf or hanging basket from which to suspend its runners, and a position in good light or gentle shade. It will tolerate temperatures as low as 40°F (5°C), and should be watered well when it is dry. Feed monthly in summer and repot annually in spring or summer. Propagation is by removal of the young plants in summer. Pot them up individually in 3-in (8-cm) containers. If the runners turn dry and crisp before the plantlets are a reasonable size, the air is too dry. Daily misting will help.

Scindapsus (Devil's ivy)

Similar to the Sweetheart plant (*Philodendron*) in appearance, *Scindapsus aureus* has the advantage of being variegated with bright yellow.

Keep the plant warm in a minimum temperature of 50°F (10°C) and in good but indirect light. Train the stems up a tripod of canes or some other support, or allow them to trail. Let the compost dry out a little between waterings and feed every two weeks in summer. Keep the compost a little drier in winter. Daily misting will prevent the leaves from turning brown. Propagate by stem cuttings in summer.

Tradescantia (Wandering sailor; Wandering jew; Spiderwort)

The wandering sailor or wandering jew is a plant for the least skilful of indoor gardeners. Its trailing stems are clothed with oval leaves that are attractively variegated pink or white, and it is extremely easy to grow. Give it good light and allow the compost to dry out between waterings. A temperature between 45–75°F (7–24°C) will suit it and it can be repotted annually in spring. Stem cuttings root readily in compost or jam jars of water.

Below: Easy to grow and easy to propagate, the Wandering sailor is available in assorted variegations.

Right: Devil's ivy (on the left), *Rhoicissus* 'Ellen Danica' (top right) and the Creeping fig (bottom right) look well grouped together with stone cider flagons.

The Ti tree is easy to grow, architecturally pleasing and relatively cheap to buy.

Right: Devil's ivy (top), zebrina (left) and *Rhoicissus* 'Ellen Danica' (right) grouped in a wicker plant stand.

Yucca (Ti tree; Spanish bayonet)

These plants have made their mark over the past five years or so and seem to be sold by every supermarket and multiple store. They usually consist of an upright plume of stiff, spiky leaves at the top of a grey-brown trunk, and although they could not be described as handsome, they are quite spectacular.

Yucca aloifolia and *Y. elephantipes* are the two most commonly available species, and both enjoy a position in a cool room with a minimum temperature of 45°F (7°C) and in brilliant light. Water generously when the compost dries out, and repot in a John Innes or another loam-based compost every two or three years. Feed every two weeks in summer. The plant can stand outdoors through the summer, and propagation is by the removal of offsets which may appear at the base of the trunk.

Zebrina (Wandering sailor)

Very similar to *Tradescantia* in appearance, the maroon and silver striped *Zebrina pendula* requires similar conditions but a slightly warmer minimum temperature of 55°F (13°C). It is superb in hanging baskets and pots and can be propagated in the same way as its commoner cousin.

Popular Flowering House Plants

Anthurium (Flamingo flower; Tail plant)

Few plants can rival the flamingo flower for spectacular brilliance when in bloom. The oval green leaves show off to perfection the lipstick-red flowers which consist of a waxy, oval spathe topped with an orange spike or spadix. The plant grows about 18 in (45 cm) high and flowers at any time between late winter and midsummer. *Anthurium scherzerianum* is the easiest kind to grow. It likes a warm, humid atmosphere (so stand the pot in a tray of moist peat or gravel) and good but indirect light. Maintain a minimum temperature of 55°F (13°C). Do not allow the compost to dry out – instead keep it moist, but not soggy, at all times. A daily spray with tepid water will keep the plant in peak condition. Feed monthly from May to September, and repot when overcrowded in spring using a peat-based potting compost. Propagation is by division at planting time.

The Flamingo flower needs humidity if it is to produce its stunning blooms.

The pink and white flowers of the Shrimp plant are produced almost all the year round.

Aphelandra (Zebra plant)

Worth growing both in and out of flower, the zebra plant has glossy green leaves heavily veined with rich creamy yellow. The bright yellow flower spikes appear like cockades at the top of the 1-ft (30-cm) stems in summer.

So often the plant loses its lower leaves after being in the house for some time. Avoid this by placing it in good but indirect light and maintaining a minimum temperature of 55°F (13°C). Mist the foliage daily in summer and keep the compost *gently* moist at all times. Feed every two weeks from May to September. Remove all faded flowers and repot the plant in spring using a peat-based compost. Propagation is by stem cuttings in early summer. These need to be kept warm at all times.

Right: Bright yellow cockades and cream-striped leaves make the Zebra plant doubly attractive.

Beloperone (Shrimp plant)

The foliage of this easy-to-grow house plant is nothing remarkable, but that hardly matters, for it is smothered in its arching dusky pink flower tails for most of the year. The pink bracts surround the true flowers which are white and hooded.

The shrimp plant likes good light and even enjoys full sun. It tolerates temperatures as low as 45°F (7°C) but prefers something a little warmer if possible. Soak the compost as soon as it feels dry, and feed the plant every

Few flowers contain
so many colours as
those of billbergia –
an easy plant to
grow in reasonable
light.

two weeks from April to October. In time, it will reach a height of 2 ft (60 cm) or so, but is best pinched in its youth to make it bushy and flower-productive. An annual cutting back to within a few inches of soil level is advisable in spring if the plant is to be retained. Repot at the same time. Alternatively, cuttings can be rooted in spring and summer and grown on to replace the ageing parent.

Billbergia (Queen's tears)

This spectacular and easily-grown plant of the pineapple family deserves to be more widely grown than it is at present. The long, thin, spiky green leaves make an upright fountain of growth and they are decorated in early summer with pendulous multicoloured flowers that droop from bright pink bracts. The plant grows to a height of around 1 ft (30 cm).

Give it a spot in good light and keep the compost gently moist through the summer, watering it when it is rather drier in winter. It will tolerate bright sunshine for part of the day. Temperatures down to 40°F (5°C) are tolerated, and feeding every two weeks in summer is enjoyed.

Repot and divide the plant in spring or summer when it is out of flower and has become overcrowded. Remove the flower stems as soon as they have faded.

Campanula (Star of Bethlehem; Bellflower)

There is only one campanula grown with any frequency as a house plant and that is the lovely *Campanula isophylla*, a trailing plant with pale blue or white wide-faced bells that are carried with amazing generosity right through summer and into autumn.

The plant likes good light, but constant bright sun will cause the flowers to fade quickly. It does not need high temperatures, but maintain a minimum of 40°F (5°C) in winter to keep it frost free. Water well when dry, and feed every two weeks in summer. In autumn the plant can be clipped right back to compost level with a pair of scissors and in spring the new shoots will appear. Divide and repot the plant at this time (or take cuttings) to increase your stock. This plant is especially good in hanging baskets.

Citrus (Orange tree)

Plant the pips of your orange if you like, but remember to be patient and not to expect Jaffas if the plants ever manage to fruit. It is far better to get hold of a plant of the Calamondin orange, *Citrus mitis*; for although the oranges are no more than 1½ in (3 cm) diameter, they are generously produced all over the plant which is green, bushy and anything up to 3 ft (1 m) and more high. The plant will bear delightfully scented white flowers before the fruits.

This orange likes good light and moderate temperatures and it can stand outdoors from June to August where it will enjoy the summer air. Maintain a minimum winter temperature of 45°F (7°C). Give the plant a good soak when the compost feels dry, and mist occasionally in summer, especially when the flowers are open for this will encourage fruit setting. Feed every two weeks from May to September, and repot in spring if necessary. Propagation is by means of stem cuttings which can be rooted in a warm place in summer. The fruits, by the way, are edible but rather bitter. However, they crystallize well and make good marmalade.

The Star of Bethlehem trails its masses of blooms to good effect in a hanging basket.

Left: The Calamondin orange is not difficult to fruit, and it can even be grown outdoors in summer. Here it is with the rubber plant (back left), a philodendron (back right), saintpaulias and a sweetheart plant.

Right: A pretty little pot plant, the Cigar plant is very easy to grow and needs very little space.

Thick glossy leaves edged with cream look good all the year round on the variegated variety of *Hoya carnosa*.

Cuphea (Cigar plant)

This delightful miniature will fit in any room. It grows to a height of 1 ft (30 cm) at maximum and decorates its upright stems with tubular red flowers tipped with deepest purple and grey. It enjoys a moderately heated room with a minimum temperature of 45°F (7°C) and good light, even full sun. Keep the compost gently moist through the summer but allow it to dry out a little more between waterings in winter. Cut the plant back to pot-rim level in spring to encourage new shoots, and divide and repot at the same time to increase your stock. Feeding every two weeks in summer is appreciated. Cuttings can be rooted in spring and summer.

Hoya (Wax flower)

There are two hoyas commonly grown as house plants: *Hoya bella* makes a small arching bush with neat green leaves carried thickly on its stems and waxy white flower clusters may appear in summer; *Hoya carnosa* is a climber with questing stems and larger leaves which also appear to be made of wax. The large flower clusters are similar to those of *H. bella* and in both, the individual white blooms are centred with purple. A variegated form of *H. carnosa* in which the leaves are splashed with cream, is freely available.

Both plants enjoy good light (full sun for part of the day at least), and warm rooms with a minimum temperature of 55°F (13°C). Give a good watering when the surface of the compost feels dry. Feed every two weeks from May to September.

Hoya carnosa will need a wire hoop or some trelliswork over which its stems can be trained. Never remove old flower heads, for the stubby stems that carry them will carry more flowers in future years. Repot in John Innes compost or another loam-based compost only when absolutely necessary, and increase by cuttings of firm shoots in spring.

Impatiens (Busy Lizzie; Balsam; Patience plant)

Here is a plant that owes its success to two of its characteristics: firstly, it is seldom out of flower; and secondly it is extremely easy to propagate for the cuttings root easily in jam jars of water. Well-grown plants will reach a height of 2 ft (60 cm) and more and may be as much across. The blooms may be white, pink, scarlet, orange or magenta, and the leaves green, green and cream or maroon.

Give your Busy Lizzie a spot in good light, but not too much direct sun or dehydration is likely, and a generous potful of compost at all times. Feed every two weeks in summer and soak the compost as soon as it feels dry. Cut back the stems to leave just a few inches of growth each spring and repot at the same time. Pinch in the early stages of growth to make a bushy plant, but stop in late spring to allow flower formation.

Right: An impressive display of flowers on the plain-leaved hoya.

Below: Given a good-sized pot and plenty of light there is no reason why the Busy Lizzie, or impatiens, should not be in flower all through the year.

Pelargonium (Geranium)

Bright flowers of red, pink, salmon, white, orange or magenta, and often
multicoloured leaves, give superb value for money to the indoor gardener
who buys a geranium. There are masses of varieties to choose from, most
of them excellent, and all are happiest in bright sunshine and temperatures
that remain above 40°F (5°C). In shade or indirect light the plants will
become spindly and yellow-leaved. Water the compost well when it is dry
and keep the plants continually on the dry side in winter. Many varieties
(especially singles) bloom all the year round. In their early stages of growth
the young plants should have their shoot tips removed to encourage
bushiness, and all faded leaves and flowers should be removed.

The zonal types will reach a height of 1 ft (30 cm) or more. The regals
grow even larger, and the ivy-leaved varieties can be allowed to trail or
trained to cover a small trellis. Yet more varieties have scented leaves, for
which they are grown rather than for their insignificant flowers.

Cuttings can be rooted in spring and summer and old plants replaced by
young ones. Good light is essential through the winter if the plants are not
to become tall and leggy. Feed them every two weeks through the summer.
The common geranium can be cut back to about 4 in (10 cm) in October,
watered occasionally during the winter to keep it alive, and the shoots
taken as cuttings in spring. Alternatively, the plants can be repotted in
spring and grown on for another year.

African violets, or saintpaulias, are available in a wide variety of colours with single flowers (bottom) or double ones (top).

Saintpaulia (African violet)
The African violet has won itself a place on many windowsills thanks to its compact rosette of leaves and its willingness to produce clusters of pink, white, purple or magenta flowers at any time of year provided it is given the treatment it likes. It enjoys bright light, so a windowsill is ideal, provided that the plant is brought inside the curtains at night. The plant should be watered from below when the pot feels light, indicating dryness. If watered from above, the leaves may be splashed and the crown encouraged to rot, so place the pot in a bowl of water for half an hour when it is dry to allow the compost to take up what it needs.

Pick off dead flowers and leaves to prevent rotting, and feed every two weeks in summer with diluted tomato fertilizer which will encourage flowering. Standing the plant on a tray of moist peat or gravel will provide it with welcome humidity. Repot the plant every other spring in a peat-based potting compost, and propagate by means of leaf cuttings which can be inserted (with their stalks) around the edge of a pot of compost or in a rooting bag. With both cuttings and mature plants maintain a minimum temperature of 60°F (16°C).

Schlumbergera (Christmas cactus)

Also known as *Zygocactus*, this plant is at its most spectacular around the Christmas period when cerise flowers sprout from the ends of its pendant stems. It looks fine in a pot placed on a well-lit windowsill which does not receive scorching sun, but is seen to best advantage when planted in a hanging basket.

When the plant is in bud it should be watered to keep the compost just moist at all times and stood in a place where it will not be disturbed: frequent movement will lead to the buds falling. Maintain a minimum temperature of 55°F (13°C). When the flowers fade, keep the plant cool and allow the compost to dry out completely between waterings. Through the summer it will benefit from being kept outdoors. Feed from June to September at two-week intervals. Occasional spraying with water will be enjoyed, and repotting can be carried out after flowering using a John Innes potting compost or another loam-based compost. Stem cuttings can be rooted in summer.

At one time the Christmas cactus was available in just one colour – cerise. Now there are many shades to choose from like this one in lilac pink.

Stephanotis (Madagascar jasmine; Clustered wax flower)

The deliciously scented white and waxy blooms of the Madagascar jasmine may appear on the twining stems at any time from late spring to autumn, and can be seen readily if the plant is trained over a small trellis or wire hoop.

Maintain a minimum temperature of 55°F (13°C) and keep the plant in good but indirect light. Avoid moving it once the flower buds have formed or they may be shed. Water well as soon as the surface of the compost begins to feel dry and spray the foliage with tepid water every day or two. Repot every other year in spring using John Innes or a soilless potting compost. As the flowers fade the stems can be shortened by up to half their length to encourage new growth and to keep the plants within bounds. Feed every two weeks in summer. Propagation is by stem cuttings rooted in warmth during the summer. Scale insects and mealy bug are common pests which should be treated as soon as they are seen.

Streptocarpus (Cape primrose)

Although the long, downy leaves of this plant are not exactly elegant, the superb flowers which appear on graceful stems above the rosette of foliage make all the waiting worthwhile. They may be lavender blue, pink, magenta, white or purple and are usually contrastingly marked in the throat. They may appear from late spring to autumn, so the plant is not without flowers for very long.

The Cape primrose does like to be kept reasonably warm in a minimum temperature of 55°F (13°C) and enjoys good but indirect light. Water well as soon as the compost feels dry. When the leaf rosette is well developed the pot will have to be weighed in the hand to detect dryness and then watered from below. Feed every two weeks in summer and repot in spring into a peat-based compost. The plant likes growing in shallow containers, so use 'half-pots' if possible. These are the same diameter but only half as deep as ordinary pots. Propagation is by division of the clumps in spring or by leaf cuttings rooted in warmth in spring and summer.

Gift Plants

Calceolaria (Slipper flower)

Brightly-coloured pouch-like flowers of yellow, white, red or orange, contrastingly spotted with deeper shades, appear in mounds on top of the foliage of the Slipper flower in spring. The plants should be kept in a cool room but in bright light. Keep the compost just moist at all times and plunge the pot in a tray of moist peat or gravel. The plants may be anything from 6–18 in (15–45 cm) high and will last several weeks in flower. They are best discarded when the blooms fade. To raise the plants in quantity, the dust-fine seeds should be sown on the surface of a peat-based seed compost and kept warm before and after germination. Greenfly can be a great problem on these plants. Spray the foliage at the first sign of attack but select the chemical carefully, making sure that it is suitable for use on this sensitive plant.

Although it is relatively short lived, the calceolaria will repay your kindness amply with dense heads of colourful pouches, often spotted with a contrasting colour.

Capsicum (Ornamental pepper)

Bright berries make a pleasant change from bright flowers, and the pointed fruits of the ornamental pepper can be had in a variety of shades. Many of them start off cream, becoming flushed with purple and orange before turning bright scarlet. White flowers appear before the fruits, making the plant of interest from late summer until January.

Keep the plant in good light, water it well when the compost is dry, and maintain a cool atmosphere with a minimum temperature of $45°F$ ($7°C$). Feed monthly in summer and spray the open flowers with water to encourage fruit setting. Dispose of the plant after flowering, but retain a few berries. You can dry these and sow the seeds to raise your own plants.

Chrysanthemum

To the disapproval of purists, the chrysanthemum is now available in bloom all the year round, thanks to the efforts of growers who have discovered the secrets of encouraging and discouraging the formation of flowers. Dwarfing compounds are also used to produce small plants that are easily accommodated indoors. Plant out the chrysanthemum in the garden at the end of its flowering period and if it survives, you will see that it grows much taller in the following year – the chemical influence having worn off.

'Pot mums', as the dwarfs are called, are available in shades of yellow, orange, red, pink, magenta and white. Give them a good soaking when the surface of the compost starts to dry, and place them in good light. They enjoy cool rooms with a minimum temperature of 45°F (7°C), but will tolerate a little warmth. High temperatures will shorten the flowering season.

Always buy a chrysanthemum which has a few flowers open. If the plant is in tight bud it may fail to bloom satisfactorily.

Cyclamen

A familiar plant at Christmas time when it is handed over as a welcome gift, the cyclamen is often a sorry sight after a week or two. The fleshy marbled leaves and pink, white, red or magenta flowers can only be kept in good condition if the plant is kept *cool*. It does not like central heating or draughts and should be watered from below when a watering can is unable to penetrate the rosette of leaves. Water when the surface of the compost is dry to the touch or when the pot feels light. Stand the pot on a tray of moist gravel to keep the atmosphere buoyant.

Keep the plant in good indirect light and feed it every two weeks when it is in bud or flower. When the flowers fade watering is usually stopped altogether and the leaves allowed to die down. The fat corm can be knocked out of its pot the following July or August and potted up in fresh compost. Start to water and encourage the plant to grow again. Alternatively discard the plant after flowering and buy a fresh one the following winter.

Below: The secret of growing the cyclamen well is to keep it cool and give it a spot in good light.

Overleaf: Plants continue to be popular gifts at Christmastime. Poinsettias (centre) are available in shades of pink and creamy-white as well as the usual bright red.

Hydrangeas are excellent house plants for cool rooms where their massive mopheads will last for many weeks.

Euphorbia (Poinsettia)

No house plant can surpass the brilliance of the poinsettia which has become a firm Christmas favourite. The bright leafy bracts remain well-coloured for several months under the right conditions, and apart from the customary vivid red, varieties are offered with pink or white bracts. The true flowers are the small yellow dots at the centre of each rosette of bracts, which are really coloured leaves.

When you buy the poinsettia (usually between November and January) it will be quite stocky for, like the pot chrysanthemum, it will have been treated with a dwarfing compound to restrict its upward growth. Keep the plant for a long time and it will eventually grow up to 3 ft (1 m) or so.

Poinsettias like to be reasonably warm and prefer a minimum temperature of 55°F (13°C). Keep them in good light – as near to a window as possible – and out of draughts. When the surface of the compost feels dry, give the plant a good watering and then wait until the compost is dry once more. An occasional spray with a hand mister will keep the plant happy.

Normally the plants are discarded when the bracts fade, but they can be grown on as a green foliage plant. Simply cut the stems right back to about 4 in (10 cm) in spring to encourage new shoots to grow. The plant can be repotted at the same time. To form its red bracts the poinsettia needs 'short days' which can be provided by placing the plant in a dark cupboard at six o'clock each evening from late September until late November. Take the plant out some time after eight o'clock the following morning and repeat this process every night! By Christmas your plant should be nicely coloured, but remember that it will be much taller than those offered in the shops, for the growth retardent will have worn off.

Feed the plant every two weeks through the summer, and propagate it by stem cuttings when it is cut down in spring. Keep the milky sap away from your eyes and mouth and wash your hands thoroughly afterwards.

Fuchsia

Pendant flowers in an assortment of shades from pink to scarlet, cerise, magenta, purple and white are carried on bushy or trailing plants, depending on the variety chosen. The plant is supremely graceful in its

arching habit, but sometimes it sheds its blooms rather too easily when grown as a house plant. Avoid this by soaking the compost as soon as it shows any sign of drying out, by not moving the plant once the buds are forming, and by keeping it in good but indirect light. Temperatures between 50–65°F (10–18°C) suit it best and it likes cool rooms rather than hot ones.

Treat them kindly and these plants will flower from spring until autumn. They lose their leaves late in the year and should be kept on the dry side and their stems cut back to around 4 in (10 cm). In spring repot the plant and then cut back to healthy shoots which are appearing from around soil level. Pinch out the tips of these in their early stages to encourage a bushy habit. Feed every two weeks from April to September and propagate by stem cuttings in spring and summer. The trailing varieties look superb in hanging baskets.

Hydrangea

For cool rooms these are good bold-flowered pot plants with mop-heads of white, pink or blue flowers that are held over fleshy green leaves. They will grow to a height of 2–3 ft (60 cm to 1 m) and bloom in spring and summer.

They demand good indirect light and constantly moist compost during their flowering period, but afterwards the compost can be allowed to dry out a little between waterings. Maintain temperatures between 45–65°F (7–18°C). Many varieties can be 'blued' by watering them with a solution of hydrangea colorant which will induce the flowers to turn a rich shade of blue. In hard water areas the plants may become yellow-leaved; this should be avoided by watering with rainwater.

Stand the plants outdoors when they have finished flowering, and cut back the stems to around 9 in–1 ft (23–30 cm). At this stage the plant can be repotted and encouraged to produce new stems through the rest of the summer. Bring indoors again in September but keep cool and in good light. Water carefully through the winter, being more generous as spring approaches. The stems carrying the flowers will need supporting individually with thin canes which can be pushed into the compost before the stems are gently tied to them. Feed every two weeks in summer and propagate by stem cuttings, also in summer.

Primula

There are three types of primula commonly offered as house plants. The most common is *Primula obconica* which bears large heads of pink, magenta, blue or white flowers over coarse green leaves. It forms a rounded plant up to 9 in (23 cm) high and carries its flowers intermittently almost right through the year, but most freely in spring. Beware of this plant if you have sensitive skin, for its leaves can cause an irritating rash. Safer is *P. malacoides*, a daintier species which has smaller leaves and finely cut flowers carried in tiers on upright stems. They may be magenta, pink or white and are sometimes delightfully scented. The polyanthus, *P. vulgaris*, is often sold in pots in spring and once it has finished blooming it can be planted in the garden where it will grow to provide its blue, red, orange, yellow or white flowers in succeeding years.

One of the daintiest primulas, *Primula malacoides* has bright blooms which are often scented.

Right: *Primula obconica* is the commonest of the indoor primulas and the longest lasting.

All these plants demand excellent light and cool temperatures of between 50–65°F (10–18°C) and should be watered when the surface of the compost feels dry. Feed them every two weeks during their flowering season. Remove any faded flowers from *P. vulgaris* but discard *P. obconica* and *P. malacoides* after flowering. New plants are best bought in, but the ambitious indoor gardener can sow seeds in early summer.

Rhododendron (Azalea)

The spectacle of a well-shaped azalea smothered in fat, promising buds has tempted many a gardener to buy a plant at Christmas time. Sadly, if the plant has not been provided with the conditions it likes, the buds will turn brown and fall, or simply stay on the plant and rot. But provide the simple environment the plant enjoys and you will not be disappointed.

First, keep it cool. Do not allow temperatures to rise above 60°F (16°C) if possible, and keep the plant in good light but not bright sunshine which may scorch the flowers. *Never* let the compost in the pot dry out. To make sure that it stays really moist, soak the pot and compost in a bucket of water every day for half an hour.

Buy a plant which has plenty of buds that are just opening, and one or two flowers that are already open. There are plenty of colours to choose from – pinks, white, salmons, reds, megentas and bi-colours, but if bought in tight bud not only will you find it difficult to tell what colour the flowers are, but they may never open in the home. Once the flowers fade, pick them off individually, and when the flowering period comes to an end either discard the plant or take a chance and plant it in the garden. With plenty of moist peat worked around its rootball it may survive to bloom outdoors in future years, though it will probably succumb to frost in hard winters.

Senecio (Cineraria)

The lovely daisy flowers of this plant are a welcome sight in winter and spring when their freshness brings a promise of things to come. The blooms may be blue, pink, white, magenta or red and many of the darker shades are contrastingly decorated with white. The flowers are held in generously-sized heads on top of the pointed green leaves, and plants are usually about 1 ft (30 cm) high.

Sadly the cineraria is not that easy to grow well, especially in homes with central heating, but its reasonable price makes a gamble worthwhile. The most important thing to do is keep it really cool and away from radiators and draughts. It also needs good but indirect light.

Cinerarias are not the easiest of gift plants to keep, but they are among the brightest.

Right: The gloxinia, with its downy green leaves and large trumpets of red, white, purple or pink can be dried off after flowering and started into growth again the following spring.

Watering is tricky: give the plant too much and it wilts never to recover; give it too little and it wilts, shortening the life of the flowers. The secret of success is to feel the surface of the compost daily and to water well when it is just dry to the touch. Standing the pot on a tray of moist peat or gravel will help to keep the leaves in good condition.

Enjoy the blooms while you can, for the plant must be discarded after flowering. New ones can be raised from seeds sown in summer but in the home this is tricky and it may be best to buy in new plants each year.

Sinningia (Gloxinia)
Gloxinias provide a real touch of the exotic for very little trouble. The rosette of downy green leaves is topped with many fat flower buds that burst to reveal wide-faced blooms of red, violet, white or pink – the darker shades usually being edged with white. Buy a plant with plenty of buds on it, and keep it in a warm room of 60–65°F (16–18°C) and in good but indirect light. Water the plant when the surface of the compost feels dry.

The flowers will emerge in summer and the plant should remain interesting for many weeks. An occasional feed during the flowering period will be beneficial, and the plant can be stood on a tray of moist gravel or peat so that the air around it remains humid.

When the flowers fade let the plant dry out completely between waterings, and as soon as the leaves begin to look sad, cease watering altogether and allow the plant to die down. The tuber can be knocked out of the pot as soon as the leaves are crisp, and stored in a cool, dry place until spring; in spring, pot it up in peat-based potting compost, so that it is just bedded into the surface with its hollow side uppermost, and give water to encourage it into growth. If all this sounds too much like hard work, you will have to buy a new plant each year.

Solanum (Winter cherry)
The Winter cherry carries hosts of round orange berries during the winter and is a popular Christmas house plant. It will grow about 1 ft (30 cm) high and the berries are preceded by white flowers with yellow centres.

All this plant demands is a sunny windowsill and reasonably cool temperatures of between 50–60°F (10–16°C). Soak the compost as soon as it feels even slightly dry to the touch, and give the plant a daily misting with a hand sprayer. If the leaves turn yellow, add a teaspoonful of Epsom salts (magnesium sulphate) to 1 pint (600 ml; US 2½ cups) of water and soak the compost with this solution once a month.

When the fruits are past their best and start to wrinkle, cut the plant back to a height of 4 in (10 cm) or so and repot in John Innes compost or another loam-based compost. Stand the plant outdoors through the summer and continue to spray it regularly with water. Feed every two weeks from May to September. Bring the plant back inside during September and enjoy it for a second year. Propagation is by seeds sown in spring, or by cuttings taken in spring and early summer.

Landscaping with House Plants

There are great possibilities for imaginative and effective house plant groupings, just as there are in the garden with hardy plants, but for the impecunious indoor gardener, or the bedsit dweller with little or no room to spare, one single house plant can add life, colour and artistry.

SPECIMEN PLANTS Instead of falling into the trap of buying a plant and then finding a space for it, try to select a plant with a particular space in mind. Use a tape measure to calculate just how much room is available, allowing for growth, and go along to the nursery or garden centre with the shape in mind. Is a tall, upright plant required, or something more bushy? Remember to make sure that the light requirement of the plant will be met in the spot in question, and also bear in mind the background for you will want to show off the plant to best effect.

If the plant pot (whether clay or plastic) fits into your room's colour scheme, all you will need is a saucer to prevent moisture marks from appearing on polished furniture and to contain surplus water after visits with the can. If the pot is clearly not a thing of beauty, then invest in a pot-holder or 'cache-pot' to mask its ugliness. China and plastic cache-pots are available in wide variety and both have the advantage of being water-proof. If you use something like a wickerwork waste paper bin, do remember to line the inside with polythene or to place a bowl in the base to catch surplus water. Make sure that any cache-pot is of a scale that is suitable for the plant it holds, and that its colour tones in rather than stands out. It is the plant that people should notice, not its container.

Plants that enjoy a moisture-enriched environment, and there are many, will be kept fresh and happy if their pots stand on a tray of moist gravel or peat. Ordinary tin trays can be used, or purpose-built plastic trays that are slightly deeper. Spread the gravel or peat over the tray to a depth of 1–2 in (2.5–5 cm) and moisten it every day or two with a hand mister or a small watering can fitted with a sprinkler head or 'rose'. As the water evaporates it will humidify the air and prevent the plant's leaves from drying out.

Trailing plants need to be given ample room to display their pendant stems. Wall-mounted pots or pot holders can be positioned in spots where the plant being grown will have suitable conditions and a plain background

Look upon bowl arrangements like this one as temporary features. Replace one or more of the plants as they go out of flower or start to look unhappy.

Plants stood together like this always seem to grow well, and can be regularly regrouped for a change of scene.

against which to be seen. Both trailers and bushy specimen plants can stand on tall plant stands or wine tables which can be repositioned at will, so long as the plant does not mind being moved around from time to time.

PLANT GROUPS Plants arranged in groups not only look good but seem to grow better as a result of each other's company, provided they are carefully selected. All should be capable of coping with the conditions prevalent in the part of the room where they are positioned. In other words, if the corner is shady all the plants must be able to tolerate low light intensity. The temperature should also be suitable for their growth.

If the plants are simply stood together, pot by pot, then there need be no worries about watering, for each one can be individually catered for. But if the plants are knocked out of their pots and planted in a bowl or trough together, then they should all have a similar moisture requirement or disaster will result.

A good solution is to arrange the plants in a suitable formation on top of a 6-in (16-cm) deep bowl or tray of moist peat, and then to bed the pots into the surface so that only the rims protrude. In this way each plant can be watered separately, and yet drying out will be slower – an advantage whatever the species.

Gift plants can easily be incorporated in such arrangements, for as soon as they fade they can be lifted out and replaced with another gift plant or something a little longer lasting. Similarly, all the plants in such arrangements can be moved around without root disturbance.

Where bowl and trough arrangements are to be permanently planted, then choose either John Innes potting compost No. 2, which contains plenty of nutrients, or a peat-based counterpart. Water with great care whatever the medium, especially if the trough or bowl is not fitted with drainage holes. If this is the case it is a good idea to provide a 3-in (8-cm) deep layer of drainage material in the base of the container (pebbles or broken flower pots will do), to keep the surplus water from souring the compost.

There are now several makes of proprietary pot clusters on the market, and these can be arranged in various formations to provide decorative arrangements. 'Towerpots' are especially popular, and these hold the plants at regular intervals up a tall column. Protruding cups stick out from the sides of the column to allow the plants room to sprout outwards and also to facilitate watering. Any excess water passes down the tower and into a drip tray at the base. A new type of towerpot is now available which is described as 'self-watering'. The gardener simply tops up a reservoir in each section, and a little coloured indicator shows him when more water should be poured in. The plants help themselves to the water present in the reservoir below each tier.

In towerpots the plants must actually be planted in the unit, but in cache-pot arrangements such as 'clusterpots' they can simply be dropped into place in one of the decorative pot hiders. Units like this can be arranged in a number of different patterns, and each plant is watered individually.

Where house plants are simply being grouped on a table or other flat surface, make sure they are arranged to best effect. Tall ones should be at the back, as a general rule, and smaller types towards the front. Trailers look best if they have room to cast their stems downwards over the edge of a shelf or table top. It is important to realize that every plant has a back and a front. Look at your plants carefully and point the front forwards, unless the plant is lop-sided due to lack of light on one side. In such a case correct the leaning by frequent turning.

'Towerpots' can be joined together or separated at intervals to provide columns of flowers and foliage.

HANGING BASKETS These pendulous features are not just for use outdoors; there are now many handsome kinds designed for use in the home.

The old wire type so frequently seen outdoors is really not suitable for indoor planting. Apart from looking rather ugly when viewed at close quarters, it will also drip water on floors and furniture, unless it is painstakingly unhitched, watered and left to drain over the sink every time watering is necessary. Solid plastic bowls which are equipped with drip trays are far better. Alternatively, hanging pots can be used where small plants or plant arrangements are being grown. A drainage layer of pebbles or broken plant pots will be necessary in these containers in the same way as in any other, and then the plant or plants can be set in John Innes or a soilless potting compost. Tap the plant or plants from their pots and set them in the new compost, firming this into place around them. The top of the rootball of each plant should rest just below the surface of the new compost which, in turn, should be at least 2 in (5 cm) below the rim of the hanging basket or pot to allow for watering.

Do remember that hanging baskets and pots dry out much more rapidly than the ordinary kind. They will need checking for water daily and should be given a really good soaking when they are found to be dry. Suspend them so that they can easily be reached by the watering can spout, or else hang them on a rope pulley which can be lowered to allow watering. Occasional sprays of water from a hand mister will keep the plant arrangements fresh, and all dead leaves and blooms should be picked off regularly.

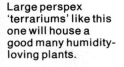

Large perspex 'terrariums' like this one will house a good many humidity-loving plants.

A plastic globe filled with compost and planted up with compact house plants.

There are many house plants suitable for planting in hanging baskets, including the following which are dealt with in this book: *Asparagus, Campanula, Chlorophytum, Fuchsia* (pendulous varieties), *Hedera helix, Hoya bella, Nephrolepis, Pelargonium* (ivy-leaved varieties), *Philodendron scandens, Saxifraga, Schlumbergera, Scindapsus, Tradescantia, Zebrina.*

BOTTLE GARDENS AND TERRARIUMS In rooms which are otherwise rather inhospitable to plant growth due to the prevalence of draughts and the lack of strong sunlight, terrariums and bottle gardens open up new avenues of plant cultivation. In the sheltered and humid environment to be found inside one of these containers many plants will feel at home and will grow far better than they would if positioned elsewhere in the room.

Suitable containers include goldfish bowls, brandy balloons (provided they are clear and not coloured), large acid bottles known as carboys, cider flagons and sweet jars which can be stoppered up. For wider-topped containers such as old aquariums some sort of cover is essential if they are

Sealed or left open, bottle gardens need very little attention once they have been planted up.

to be kept humid. Narrow-necked jars and bottles are by no means easy to plant up, but with a few easily made tools the job is not too complicated.

First of all thoroughly clean the container with detergent and water, then rinse well to remove all traces of chemicals. Allow the container to dry, or wipe it down if you can get your hand inside. Place 2 in (5 cm) of gravel in the base of the container, followed by 1 in (2.5 cm) of charcoal. The latter will prevent the compost from turning sour. Now feed in between 2–4 in (5–10 cm) of compost and either level it or arrange it in gentle contours. You can use either John Innes potting compost No. 1 or a peat-based equivalent, and if the garden is being made in a narrow-necked vessel then the gravel, charcoal and compost will have to be fed in through a home-made paper funnel. The landscaping of the compost in such vessels can be accomplished with a teaspoon taped to the end of a length of cane, and this implement will also be needed at planting time.

When the plants have been selected, decide where each one is to go and excavate a hole (with the spoon and stick if necessary). Either drop the plant through the neck of the bottle, or put it in place with your hand, firming the compost around it. A cotton reel pushed on to the end of a cane is a good firmer where the bottle neck is narrow.

Plant at a spacing which is sufficient to allow some room for growth, and do not be tempted to use rampant plants (which will quickly swamp the container, or flowering plants for the faded flowers may cause the foliage to rot.

When planting is completed, water the compost by allowing the water from a long-spouted can to run down the inside of the bottle. Wider-topped containers and aquariums can be watered more easily. Leave the planting arrangement to settle for a week or two, then seal up the bottle or place a sheet of glass over terrariums.

Occasional steaming up is inevitable, but this will be of little consequence if the container is kept out of bright sunlight which is likely to aggravate the condition and burn up the plants. Remove the cap or glass to let steamed-up containers clear, and replace it once the condensation has vanished.

Watering will be necessary very infrequently – no more than three or four times a year if the terrarium is kept out of direct light in gentle shade – and waterlogging must be guarded against at all times.

Suitable plants for terrariums and bottle gardens include: *Chamaedorea, Ficus pumila, Fittonia, Maranta, Peperomia, Pilea, Saxifraga.*

Keeping Plants Healthy

You cannot treat a house plant like a piece of furniture by dusting it occasionally and splashing a drop of water around now and again to keep it happy. There are only one or two plants that might thrive under such circumstances. House plants are living things and if they are to stay alive and bristling with health, you will have to master a few skills and understand the likes and dislikes of your horticultural room-mates.

LIGHT House plants certainly have assorted requirements when it comes to light intensity, but none of them grows in total darkness in their native habitat. Some plants do grow well in shady corners, but even here there should be enough light to read by.

By far the majority of plants need what is described as 'good indirect light'. That is, a spot which receives plenty of light from a window through which the sun does not shine directly. A south-facing window is the sunniest. Windows facing east and west will receive direct sunlight for part of the day. If a plant can be positioned so that it is protected from the direct glare, but exposed to the general brightness, then it will do well.

Where direct sunlight cannot be avoided, choose a plant which is happy to be directly lit for all or part of the day. The preferences of all the plants mentioned in this book are given under their specific headings. Turn to the chapter on *Choosing the Right Plants* to help you find the best specimen for any particular situation.

HUMIDITY Very moist air will induce fungal attack and rotting of plant tissue. Very dry air will cause flowers and leaf tips to turn brown. Somewhere between these two extremes is the happy medium that most house plants enjoy.

In centrally heated rooms which have a dry atmosphere, nearly all plants will perform better if they are stood on a tray of gravel which can be moistened regularly. The water will evaporate and surround the plants with a gently-moist atmosphere that is conducive to healthy growth. Peat is a good alternative to gravel, and if a deeper container is used for this medium, 4–6 in (10–15 cm), then the pots can be partially plunged. This not only provides additional atmospheric moisture, but also slows down the rate at which the roots dry out, so making the plant's environment more stable.

Below: Plants that like a humid atmosphere can usually be kept happy if they are grouped together on trays of moist gravel.

Overleaf: A kitchen with many suitable spots for house plants in good light and gentle shade.

Humidity of a more generous nature can be provided if plants are sprayed
with tepid water through a fine hand mister once or twice a day. Foliage
plants, in particular, benefit from this treatment. Avoid spraying open
flowers or hairy-leaved plants which may rot as a result of being coated with
water.

WATERING More house plants die from over-watering than from any other
single cause. Master the commonsense of watering and you are half way to
becoming a good indoor gardener. The vast majority of house plants should
be watered when the surface of the compost in the pot feels dry to the touch.
When it feels like a wrung-out flannel it is still moist. That is not to say a
plant should be allowed to become bone dry, but if it is kept constantly over-
moist then the compost will become sour and the roots will suffer. Plant roots
need oxygen as well as water if they are to function properly.

Soilless or peat-based composts should not be allowed to dry out to the
same extent as loam-based composts. They should be re-wetted as soon as
they feel like a wrung-out flannel.

Just to complicate matters, there are one or two plants which do like to be
moist, or even wet, at all times, but these are few and far between and are
indicated under their specific headings.

When you think that the surface of the compost is dry fill the pot to its
rim with water. Use ordinary tap water unless you live in a particularly hard
water area, in which case rainwater will be better, especially for plants such
as azaleas which may turn yellow as a result of excessive lime in the water.

Only when it is impossible to penetrate the rosette of leaves with the
spout of a watering can should a plant be watered from below. Stand the
plant in a bowl or tray of water and allow it to stay there for half an hour
before removing it and placing it in its usual position. By that time it will
have taken up what it wants.

Remember that most plants need less water in winter than they do in
spring and summer. This does not mean that they should be given less water
each time they are visited with the can, but that they can be allowed to
remain dry for longer periods of time.

FEEDING All potting compost contains nutrients, but the plant will use up
this supply in a relatively short time. For this reason additional feeding is
necessary. John Innes composts or other loam-based composts are
capable of retaining their nutrients longer than peat-based composts; plants
growing in the latter will need to be fed from eight weeks after potting, and
plants in John Innes or a soilless compost from twelve weeks onwards. Plants
should only be fed while they are in active growth which is, generally, from
April to September. Those which flower during the winter months can be
given occasional feeds at this time as well.

Liquid foods which are diluted in water are the best types to use for pot plants. Apply them as directed by the manufacturer and *never* add one for the pot. Only apply them when the compost is already moist – then they can go straight into action. In most cases liquid feeds can be applied once every two weeks, but for slower-growing and less vigorous plants, monthly applications will be sufficient. Special liquid fertilizer is made for pot plants, but tomato fertilizer is particularly beneficial to flowering plants, for it contains extra potassium and magnesium – two nutrients that encourage flower formation.

HYDROCULTURE If you are a confirmed failure where house plants are concerned and are convinced that you will never master the technique of watering, then there are units on the market that will make life amazingly easy. Known as 'hydroculture', the system incorporates a plastic reservoir and, instead of being grown in compost, the plant's roots are surrounded by a lightweight aggregate held in a perforated pot. The pot sits on top of the reservoir and the entire unit is encased in a handsome cover so that it appears to be little different from an ordinary plant in a pot. An indicator built into the side or top of the unit shows when water should be poured into the reservoir to top it up, and special soluble fertilizer can be added when

Plants such as the cyclamen which have an impenetrable rosette of leaves can be watered from below. Fill a saucer with water, stand the plant in it for half an hour and then discard any remaining water.

Always water from above if you can see the compost, and fill the pot to its rim with water.

Right: Hydroculture units are ideal for the busy indoor gardener. The plant sits in a container of aggregate which fits inside a plastic reservoir of water.

This pelargonium is obviously in need of repotting – the roots are crammed around the edge of the 'rootball' and all the food supply is exhausted.

necessary. Not only do the units make cultivation easier for the not-so-good gardener, but they also allow the busy gardener to be away from home without having to worry about the state of his house plants. Once topped up, the unit will last for several days, or even weeks in some cases.

As the plants grow they can be carefully transferred to larger hydro-culture units. Conversion kits can be bought to transfer compost-grown plants to hydroculture, but success is more likely where young plants are bought already in the units. For some unknown reason many newly acquired plants seem to settle down more quickly in the home when they are being grown on the hydroculture system than when they are planted in compost.

POTTING When a plant growing in a pot has not only exhausted the supply of nutrients but also filled the compost with its roots, then it usually requires a larger-sized container. The exceptions to this rule have already been mentioned, but most plants thrive best when they have plenty of room to spread their subterranean parts. Large plants may become top-heavy and overbalance when grown in small pots, so there is further reason for moving them on.

Never give a plant a new pot which is vastly greater in size than its previous one. An increase of 2 in (5 cm) in rim diameter will be plenty. Whether you use a clay or a plastic pot is entirely up to you. The clay type needs a layer of drainage material in the base to prevent the single hole from being blocked by compost (if John Innes mixes or other loam-based mixes are being used), but the plastic types with their many holes can be filled direct. Large pebbles, or pieces of broken flower pot laid concave side downwards, are the best drainage materials. Always soak new clay pots in water overnight before they are used; this rids them of any chemical deposits and prevents them from absorbing too much water from the compost.

Before repotting any plant, examine it to see if it really needs more room. The give-away signs are roots emerging from the drainage holes in the base of the pot, a general appearance of being starved and, if the plant is knocked out of its container, a predominance of roots on the outside of the compost against the insides of the pot.

1) If a clay pot is used, lay crocks (pieces of broken flowerpot) over the hole in the base, concave side downwards. 2) Place a little compost in the pot. 3) Sit the plant in position and fill around it with more compost, firming it with your fingers. 4) The final level of the compost in the new pot allows room for watering.

There are two main types of potting compost; those based on peat, perhaps with the addition of a little sand or some other inert medium, and those which are based on loam, to which sand and peat have been added. The first type is known as soilless or peat-based compost, and the second as loam-based compost of which John Innes is a good example. Both types contain a certain amount of fertilizer to provide the plants with the nutrition they need.

Peat-based composts should not be firmed quite so much as loam-based composts and should not be allowed to dry out completely between waterings for they will shrink and be difficult to re-wet. Nor should drainage material be placed in the bottom of pots when they are used.

Loam-based composts have the advantage of being heavier than peat-based types and will hold large plants upright more effectively. They also hold on to their nutrients for rather longer.

In no circumstances should ordinary garden soil be used for pot plants. It will not provide them with sufficient nutrition and, in the confines of a pot, will not be very hospitable to the roots.

65

Right: Twining plants will often climb better up foam-clad stakes which should be kept moist at all times.

Single-stemmed plants like this Umbrella tree can be held upright with a single bamboo cane.

To pot a plant in soilless compost, use a clean pot and place a little compost over the drainage holes in the base. Knock the plant out of its existing pot and sit it on the compost in the base of the new one. Feed the new compost around it, *lightly* firming it with your fingers or with a pointed stick if space is restricted. When potting is complete the surface of the new compost should be between $\frac{1}{2}$–$1\frac{1}{2}$ in (1–3 cm) below the rim of the new container, and the surface of the rootball should rest just below the level of the new compost. Water the plant in.

To pot a plant in John Innes compost proceed as for soilless compost, but place a layer of drainage material in the base of clay pots and firm the compost rather more. Small pot plants can be potted in John Innes potting compost No. 1; more vigorous types in John Innes potting compost No. 2, and very large plants in John Innes potting compost No. 3.

Before potting any plant make sure that it is moist at the roots, and then water it in so that it can settle down immediately. Position all newly-potted plants in a warm, lightly shaded place for a few days, and give them an occasional misting with a hand sprayer, then move them to their permanent position.

STAKING Tall plants which have stems that are too feeble or top-heavy to support themselves will need a little help. Some will enjoy leaning on a moss- or foam-covered stick *provided that this is kept moist* with the aid of a hand mister. If the moss or foam remains dry then you might just as well use an ordinary cane which is much cheaper. Push the support into the compost a few inches away from the stem and gently tie the stem to it at intervals. If the plant has aerial roots they can be lightly tied to the mossy stick where they will be able to extract moisture.

Ivies and other climbers can be trained over wire hoops and trellises rigged up above the pot and either supported by the compost or a nearby wall. The stems will usually hold on by themselves if given a few twists to start them off.

Cane tripods can be pushed into the pots of climbers if you want to create a column of foliage, and single stout canes will be fine for Rubber plants and other single-stemmed specimens.

CLEANING Do not go to the length of buying a special cleaning fluid for the leaves of your plants. Glossy types can be brought up shining if they are sponged with a mixture of milk and water, or just water if you are not worried about the gloss. Hairy-leaved plants should never be touched with a damp cloth. Instead, use a dry paint brush and flick the dust from the surface of the leaves.

PRUNING Instructions on pruning are given under the individual plant headings where they are thought to be necessary. Always use a sharp pair of secateurs (or scissors) on thin stems and always cut back to a leaf or bud. Never leave a finger of stem sticking up on its own. In their young stages, many plants need to be 'pinched out' to encourage bushiness and the production of a greater number of stems that will carry flowers and leaves. Simply nip out the tip of each stem with your finger and thumb. Shoots lower down the stem will then grow to fill out the plant. Always remove faded leaves and flowers unless the flowers are followed by berries.

WINTER CARE Always remember that most plants have a resting season during which they need no food and a reduced supply of water. With most permanent house plants, this resting season occurs in winter, and they should be allowed to go a little longer between waterings.

Plants that can tolerate shady conditions in summer will often appreciate a little more light in winter when the sun is lower in the sky and the light intensity is lower.

HOLIDAY CARE If a neighbour can water your plants while you are on holiday, then you need not worry too much about their welfare. If no one is available, you will have to devise some other means of watering. There are several ways to do this. Either bed all the plants in trays of moist peat placed in a shady room – even sun-loving plants will tolerate a lack of direct light for a week or two – or stand them on a layer of special capillary matting on your kitchen draining board. The porous matting can be taken down into the sink in which is left a bowl with some water in it. The mat draws up the water and the plants take up water from its surface. It is important that the compost in the pots comes into contact with the mat. Plastic pots present no problem here, for they have thin bases and plenty of holes through which the compost protrudes, but clay pots must be provided with wicks made from little strips of matting pushed up into the compost.

Below: Hairy-leaved plants can be brushed free of dust – use a dry paint brush.

Left: Clean the leaves of glossy plants by sponging them with moist cotton wool.

What's the Trouble?

Even the most accomplished indoor gardener will encounter problems from time to time. His plants may fall prey to insects or diseases, or some cultural mistake may result in what is technically known as a physiological disorder. Here are the most common problems, but remember that well-grown plants are far more likely to resist attacks from both pests and diseases.

DISORDERS

WILTING If the plant wilts and the soil in the pot is dry, the problem is almost certainly under-watering. Stand the pot in a bowl of water for half an hour. Continuous under-watering will lead to browning of the leaves and eventually leaf fall. Flowering plants kept too dry will fade very quickly. If the plant is wilting and the soil in the pot is moist, then the cause is likely to be over-watering. If this state of affairs continues, many of the leaves will eventually turn yellow and fall. Allow the rootball to dry out and then resume watering much more carefully. Midday sun may cause temporary wilting of plants which cannot withstand high light intensity and the consequent increase in temperature. Move such plants to indirectly lit spots.

BUD DROP When flower buds fall check that the plant has not been under-watered, that the air is not too dry, that the plant has not been moved recently, and that there is sufficient light to encourage bud development.

LEAF BROWNING There are several possible causes of leaves turning brown, but the most common are under-watering, draughts, too high a temperature, dry air, sun scorch, over-feeding and too little light. Decide which one is responsible in your particular case by a process of elimination.

LEAF FALL This is usually the result of some kind of check to growth due to a sudden change in growing conditions. Alternatively, it may be as a result of draughts, over-watering, under-watering or the plant being given a chill.

YELLOW LEAVES Do not worry if an occasional leaf at the base of the plant turns yellow and falls – this is simply due to old age. Where the problem is more widespread and a number of leaves are yellowing, the cause may be draughts, lack of light, or over-watering. When the leaves of hydrangeas and rhododendrons turn yellow, this indicates that they are suffering from lime-induced chlorosis. Use rainwater instead of tap water and apply a diluted dose of iron sequestrene to bring back their greenness.

LEAF SPOTS Brown spots on the leaves may be caused by water splashing, especially on hairy-leaved plants, or by sun scorch, over or under-watering or by a pest or disease.

SPINDLY SHOOTS Leggy stems with small leaves and pale green colouring are almost certainly due to lack of light, though under-feeding can produce stems which are lacking in vigour. Move the plant to a better lit place and give it some diluted liquid fertilizer.

PESTS

GREENFLY appear on all manner of pot plants. They suck sap, reduce vigour, secrete sticky honeydew and so encourage the growth of sooty mould, which is described on page 70. They also transmit disfiguring virus diseases. Wash small infestations off under the tap or squash them with your fingers! Larger outbreaks can be controlled by spraying with a systemic insecticide, but check that this is suitable for the plant in question. Your garden centre or nursery will advise.

WHITEFLY are to be found on the underside of leaves. They are white and 'V'-shaped and fly in circles when disturbed. They are difficult to control because the youngsters are resistant to chemical sprays, but the fact that they reduce vigour and secrete honeydew means that they should be controlled. Spray every three or four days with bioresmethrin over a period of two weeks.

Plants like this Joseph's coat will lose their lower leaves if kept short of light, or in too cool a temperature. If they are given too much or too little water the same symptoms may result.

RED SPIDER MITES are minute brown mites about the size of pinpricks. They suck the sap and bleach the leaves of plants and also spin webs around the shoots. Prevent attacks by maintaining a moist atmosphere (hand misting daily is helpful in discouraging this pest). Severe infestations can be sprayed at weekly intervals with derris or malathion.

SCALE INSECTS seem to be very fond of ferns, but they also attack other plants with glossy leaves. They adhere to the stems and usually the undersides of leaves and look like little brown lumps. They secrete honeydew and weaken the plant. Wipe off the scales with moist cotton wool and then spray with malathion to discourage further attacks. Severe outbreaks will require very painstaking removal, for insecticides have difficulty in penetrating the shell of the insect.

MEALY BUGS surround themselves with a white deposit that looks like cotton wool. They can be controlled in the same way as scale insects.

CATERPILLARS can make a real mess of plant leaves in a short time. They eat the edges and also make unsightly holes. In small outbreaks, search out the caterpillars and pick them off by hand. Larger attacks can be controlled by spraying with derris.

DISEASES

BOTRYTIS is a fungus disease which causes plant tissue to turn brown and rot, at which stage it is covered in greyish fur. This fungus also causes geranium cuttings to turn black at the base – a condition known as blackleg. To discourage botrytis, always maintain a well-ventilated rather than a stagnant atmosphere and reduce humidity if possible. Remove all faded leaves from plants, and also any parts that are infected with the disease.

The Kangaroo vine (*Cissus antarctica*) is likely to suffer from sooty mould if not kept free of greenfly. Occasional cleaning with moist cotton wool will keep the leaves shining as they are on this plant.

RUST disease attacks geraniums and is identifiable by the circular brown marks on the underside of the leaves. Where single plants are found to be infected put them straight into the dustbin and wash your hands before handling other geraniums. If many plants are affected and you cannot afford to throw them away, remove and burn all infected leaves and spray the plants with dithane.

DAMPING OFF occurs in seedlings as a result of fungal attack. The young plants keel over at ground level and rot off. Ventilation and reduction of humidity will discourage this disease, and the seedlings can be watered with a substance known as Cheshunt compound, available from horticultural sundriesmen, or an appropriate fungicide.

SOOTY MOULD is a black, sometimes downy fungus which grows on the honeydew secreted by aphids and other insect pests. It can be wiped off with moist cotton wool, but aphid control will deprive the fungus of its food and prevent infestation.

MILDEW is at the other end of the spectrum from sooty mould being white in colour and of a more powdery nature. Reduce the likelihood of attack by maintaining a free circulation of air rather than high humidity. Pick off badly infected leaves and spray severely infected plants with benomyl.

VIRUS DISEASES can cause all manner of discolorations and distortions to plant foliage. They are often transmitted by greenfly, which is why control of these insect pests is important. Plants which are severely infected with virus diseases should be discarded and under no circumstances should cuttings be taken from them, for these will also be infected. There is no way of controlling virus diseases in house plants once they are evident.

NOTES When using chemicals always spray outdoors and follow the manufacturer's instructions. Wash your hands thoroughly afterwards and store all chemicals out of the reach of pets and children.

Plant Propagation

Plant propagation does not always require a great deal of skill, and there are certain methods which even the most inexperienced of gardeners can use to make several new plants from an old one. Listed here are the most popular ways.

CUTTINGS A cutting is a portion of the plant which is removed and then encouraged to form roots (in the case of a stem or leaf cutting) or shoots (in the case of a root cutting).

Stem cuttings can be taken from all manner of house plants. They are nearly always removed in spring and summer when the chances of their rooting is greatest. They consist of 3–4 in (8–10 cm) long shoot tips which are cut horizontally just below a leaf joint. All the lower leaves are removed, to leave three or four at the top, and the cuttings are either inserted in jars of water or in small pots of cutting compost obtainable from a nursery, garden shop or garden centre. Fill a 4-in (10-cm) pot with the compost. Lightly firm it and dib in five cuttings around the edge with a pencil so that half the stem of each cutting is buried. Water the compost and then stand the pot in a warm spot which receives good but indirect light. Glossy-leaved cuttings will enjoy extra humidity and this can be provided if a polythene

Take cuttings from healthy shoots; prepare them by removing lower leaves and slicing below a leaf joint, and then insert them around the edges of a pot of cutting compost.

Right: Even woody house plants such as this azalea (*Rhododendron simsii*) can be propagated from cuttings if they are taken from the plant in late summer and rooted in a pot covered with a polythene bag. Use a peaty compost that contains no lime.

Right: Leaf cuttings of African violets (saintpaulias) can be inserted in trays of cutting compost and kept warm and moist while they root.

Above: *Begonia rex* can be propagated from leaf cuttings. Lay a healthy leaf on a tray of cutting compost and slit several of the main veins.

Above: Weigh down the leaf with small pebbles or pieces of crock so that the slit portions come into contact with the compost.

bag is held over the top of the pot with an elastic band. Check the pot for water at intervals, but do not keep the compost soggy. As soon as the cuttings start to grow, they can be knocked out of the pot and potted up individually in 3–4-in (8–10-cm) pots of John Innes potting compost No. 1 or a soilless equivalent.

Miniature growing bags which are known as rooting bags can now be purchased and they are extremely efficient at rooting cuttings. Slits are made in one side of the bag and the prepared cuttings pushed in. Water is added and replenished when necessary, and when the young plants have rooted, the bag is torn apart and the youngsters potted up.

Plants such as *Peperomias* and *Saintpaulias* can be propagated from leaf cuttings. All this involves is the removal of a leaf (with stalk) which is then dibbed into compost in the same way as a stem cutting. A young plant will emerge at the base of the leaf and can then be potted up.

Begonia rex can be propagated from leaf cuttings in a different way. Prepare a seed tray of cutting compost and then sever a mature leaf from the plant. Lay it on top of the compost and weight it down with small pebbles. Use a knife to slit some of the main veins of the leaf. Keep the compost gently moist at all times and eventually tiny plants will arise at each of the slits. Pot them up and grow them on.

Streptocarpus leaves are long and thin and can be cut laterally into short sections. Bed the bases of these into cutting compost and again wait for

Seeds can either be sown in pots or plastic seeds trays as shown here. Fill the tray with seed sowing compost.

Scrape away the excess compost and then firm and level that which remains with a home-made presser board or the bottom of a flower pot.

young plants to arise. Make sure that the cut surface nearest the base of the leaf is bedded into the compost, so that the sap is running in the right direction.

Dracaenas can be propagated by root cuttings. Knock the plant out of its pot and scrape away some of the compost around the lower part of the rootball. Large, fat roots known as 'toes' may be found, and these can be severed in 2- or 3-long (5- or 8-cm) sections and potted individually in 3-in (8-cm) pots of peaty compost. The rounded end of each toe should point downwards and the cut surface should be level with the top of the compost. Keep these cuttings warm and they will soon send up shoots. The plant from which they were taken can be repotted with no ill effects.

DIVISION This is perhaps the easiest means of house plant propagation. All it involves is the pulling apart of a mature clump-forming plant at repotting

Right: Scatter the seeds thinly and evenly either from a fold of paper or from your fingers like salt.

Overleaf: Geraniums, or pelargoniums, are easy to grow and can be stood outdoors in the summer where they will flower continuously. They can be easily propagated from cuttings.

Sieve a fine covering of compost over the seeds – stop sieving as soon as they disappear from view.

time (in spring or summer) to produce several smaller plants each with roots and shoots. Pull the plants apart with your hands if possible, or use a sharp knife for tough subjects. Pot up the new plants individually in John Innes potting compost No. 1 or a peat-based equivalent.

SEEDS Some house plants do set seeds, others can be propagated from shop-bought seeds. Fill a 4-in (10-cm) plastic pot with seed compost and lightly firm it so that the surface rests $\frac{1}{2}$ in (1 cm) below the rim of the pot. Sow the seeds thinly on top of the compost and then lightly cover with the mixture. Water gently but thoroughly. Very fine seeds should not be covered at all. Cover the pot with a small piece of glass and then a sheet of paper and put it in a warm place such as the airing cupboard. Check the pot every day and as soon as the first seedling breaks the surface, bring the pot out into a well-lit spot and remove the glass and paper.

Cover the container first with a sheet of glass and then with some newspaper. Remove and wipe the glass clear of condensation every day.

The plantlets produced at the end of Spider plant stems can be rooted either in glasses of water or small pots of cutting compost.

The rubber plant (*Ficus elastica*) often grows too tall for the home and the lower leaves may have fallen. Shorten it by air layering. 1) Make an upward incision into the stem at an angle of 45°. 2) Fill the incision with moist sphagnum moss. 3) Place more moss around the stem and then wrap with polythene. 4) Seal top and bottom with adhesive tape. When white roots can be seen through the polythene the new plant can be potted up and the old one grown on as a more bushy specimen.

When the seedlings are large enough to handle, ease them out of the compost with a pencil (keeping as much mixture around the roots as possible) and transfer them individually to 2½-in (6-cm) pots of John Innes potting compost No. 1 or a peat-based equivalent.

Water them in and grow them on, transferring them to larger pots when necessary.

AIR LAYERING When Rubber plants and Swiss cheese plants outgrow the headroom available, they can be shortened rather cunningly and the uppermost piece of stem can be turned into a new plant. Take a sharp knife and make an upward cut in the stem at a suitable point. The cut should run at an angle of around 45° so that a 1½-in (3-cm) long tongue is created. Pad this with moist sphagnum moss which is available from your florist, and wrap the stuff around the outside of the stem too. Now wrap the cut area of stem with a piece of polythene held firm top and bottom with sticky tape. It will be several months before you see any roots through the polythene, but that's when the upper section of the plant can be removed entirely and potted up on its own. The parent plant can be trimmed neatly just above a leaf, and it should then sprout new shoots which will make it nice and bushy. Cosset the newly removed plant by keeping it warm and shaded for a few weeks and then place it in its permanent spot.

PLANTLETS If complicated propagation puts you off completely, then stick to making new Spider plants and Mother-of-thousands. Both these plants produce miniatures of themselves at the ends of long stems. Detach the babies and sit them in little pots of moist compost. They will soon grow into new plants provided you stop them from drying out.

The House Plant
Grower's Calendar

SPRING
Propagate house plants by seeds, cuttings, plantlets, air layering and division.
Repot plants that have outgrown their existing containers.
Pinch out the shoot tips of young plants to encourage them to become bushy.
Buy new house plants from a reputable supplier.
Cut back old plants to produce new shoots for cuttings.
Make bottle gardens and terrariums and plant up hanging baskets.

SUMMER
Feed all actively growing plants at two-weekly or monthly intervals, and continue to take cuttings.
Stand pot plants outdoors for a while in good weather.
Water thoroughly as soon as the compost looks dry, and keep those plants that like to be constantly moist well supplied with water.
Remove all faded flowers and leaves.
Stake stems which are weak or top heavy.
Spray foliage plants daily with a hand mister if they appreciate a moist atmosphere.

AUTUMN
Begin to increase the interval between feeds.
Continue to remove faded leaves and flowers.
Pot up rooted cuttings taken in summer.
Look out for Christmas plants and buy good specimens.
Clean grime from house plant leaves.
Bring in all plants that were outdoors for the summer.

WINTER
Allow longer periods of time to elapse between visits with the watering can except where azaleas and other moisture lovers are being grown.
Stop feeding (though plants in flower can be fed once a month).
Make sure that night temperatures do not fall too low.
Guard against draughts.
Keep plants away from radiators and other heat sources.
Give plants growing in shade a spot with more light if possible.